The Private Diary
of an O.J. Juror

The Private Diary of an O.J. Juror

BEHIND THE SCENES OF THE TRIAL OF THE CENTURY

BY

Michael Knox
with **Mike Walker**

Preface by Roy Innis
National Chairman, Congress of Racial Equality

Conclusion by Pierce O'Donnell

DOVE
BOOKS

Copyright © 1995 by Dove Books

All rights reserved. No part of this book may be reproduced
or transmitted in any form or by any means, electronic or
mechanical, including photocopying, recording, or any
information storage and retrieval system, without permission
in writing from the publisher.

ISBN 0-7871-0580-5

Printed in the United States of America

Dove Books
301 North Canon Drive
Beverly Hills, CA 90210

Distributed by Penguin USA

Text design and layout by Folio Graphics Co., Inc.
Cover design and Michael Knox photo by Rick Penn-Kraus
Cover photo of O.J. Simpson: AP/World Wide Photos
Back cover courtroom illustration by Bill Robles

If you purchased this book without a cover you should be aware
that this book is stolen property. It was reported as "unsold and
destroyed" to the publisher and neither the author nor the
publisher has received any payment for this "stripped" book.

First Printing: June 1995

10 9 8 7 6 5 4 3 2 1

*To Beverly,
the kids, and Jehovah,
without whose support
none of this
would have happened.*

Acknowledgments

I'd like to thank my mother and my father, Thomas Lee and Evernell Knox, for the love and continued guidance that they have shown me throughout my life. I have had many ups and downs since 1978 but they have always been there for me. I would also like to extend a special thanks to my grandmother, Johnnie Mae Duson, who in the early years of my childhood became like a mother to me. "Mother," as we all call her, is the only person who really understands me. I lived with her on and off for several years while I was growing up in San Diego. "Mother," I can't thank you enough for the love, understanding, and support in those early days. I would also like to thank my six brothers and sisters for all of their love and support throughout the years.

I would also like to extend special thanks to my newly acquired friends at Dove, Michael Viner, who had enough faith in me and my story to see this project through, and Michael Walker, without whom I would have been unable to complete this project. I would also like to thank my attorney, Arthur Barens, who throughout this ordeal has become a very close personal friend. I'd like to thank all of my cousins in Los Angeles, especially the May family who took me in in 1985 and helped me on my way to a stable life in Los Angeles. And, last but not least, I'd like to thank Kurt Benjamin, a true friend, an entrepreneur, without whom this book may never have been written.

Foreword by Mike Walker

The O.J. jury has made legal history. So has Michael Knox, who successfully challenged California's outrageous new law that says witnesses and jurors in criminal cases cannot tell their stories if they profit by so much as a penny.

Any journalist who believes fiercely in our First Amendment freedoms of speech and of the press would be proud to know Michael Knox. He's an unpretentious man who suddenly found himself caught up in a story that's riveted America, even the world. And any journalist I know would have leaped at the chance to write this book.

Lightning rarely strikes twice for a journalist on the same story. I am incredibly fortunate to co-author this important and intriguing book with Michael Knox so soon after publishing the most famous book about the case, *Nicole Brown Simpson: Private Diary of a Life Interrupted*, with Faye Resnick. It may not be unprecedented for a journalist to get two great angles on one world-class story, but it surely is rare. My thanks to Michael Knox and Michael Viner, the publisher, for their confidence.

The deadline pressure was extreme. As juror after juror was excused from the case, many legal experts predicted a mistrial. As I write this, Judge Ito has just removed two more jurors in the aftermath of Francine Florio-Benten's dismissal. Every story has its own time to be told, and it's time to answer the questions being asked in the wake of this unheard of jury attrition and the first-ever revolt of an American jury.

It should be noted that every effort was made to protect the identities of the jurors still sitting on the case. Every incident and every character trait is true and no-holds-barred. But to preserve anonymity while the trial is in progress, the authors assigned arbitrary names and juror numbers to each sitting juror. They—and you—will recognize each and every one at the end of the trial. The names of dismissed jurors are their own, of course, but juror numbers are also arbitrary.

One thing that struck me as I worked on my second book about this high-profile case: It's no surprise that a recent poll shows that a majority of Americans disapprove of the press. Working with Faye Resnick, and now Michael Knox, and watching my fellow journalists come barreling at them with pens and cameras blazing, I've felt the power of the press from a whole new perspective.

I've been quoted as saying the press should be scrutinized just as ruthlessly as we scrutinize others, and bashed vigorously whenever we're rude, arrogant or—even worse—wrong. My position hasn't changed, but I'll add one more thing: We've got to be more careful about coming to stories with preconceived notions just because we're under deadline pressure. I fielded phone inquiries from fellow journalists from as far away as Europe who were pursuing an outrageous rumor about Michael Knox and his relationship with a female juror. You'll learn more about it in the book—but strong denials and a total lack of evidence kept the rumor out of print and off the air.

A final note: As I write this in Beverly Hills, my phone rings and it is Michael Viner, publisher of Dove Books, who tells me that Judge Ito has subpoenaed him to appear in his chambers. This is the newer, calmer Judge Ito. The last time I wrote a book he stopped the trial.

—Mike Walker
Hotel Nikko, Beverly Hills
June 1, 1995

Preface by
Roy Innis

"All art is but imitation of nature."
—SENECA

When the O.J. Simpson saga burst upon the scene, my mind shifted instantly to a recent performance of Giuseppe Verdi's Opera, *Otello,* and to the last time I enjoyed a production of William Shakespeare's *Othello.* Like so many before me, I have not escaped the inevitable temptation to compare these great works of art. The O.J. Simpson saga adds a new dimension to that debate, for here real life rivals art. Neither of these great works, Verdi's nor Shakespeare's, surpasses the drama of O.J. Simpson in sustained theater and social relevance. This confirms the observation of the ancient Roman philosopher Seneca that "all art is but imitation of nature."

The story of today's moor, our "Lion of Venice," cannot be viewed detached from ourselves, as is possible with the great works of Shakespeare and Verdi. O.J. Simpson's story transcends the boundaries imposed on literature and music; it is a living microcosm of our society. It has had a far-reaching effect on individuals and institutions that have intersected (directly and indirectly) with it: media, police, judges, lawyers, jurors, and ordinary citizens.

From the start of the O.J. Simpson crisis, the media and their legal analysts have operated with little restraint and without a sense of proportion. The Los Angeles Police Department and forensic investigators were demonized beyond all reason. Past police misconduct and atrocities, like the brutal beating of Rodney King, were dredged up. These were presented to the public as if no change had been made in the management of the Los Angeles Police Department, or that a new chief, a black man, had replaced Daryl Gates. Willie Williams, the new chief, and his administration were impugned along with Daryl Gates and the old Los Angeles Police Department. The worst devils in lawyers were conjured up in this case. The human failings of judges were exposed. But it is the effect on the ordinary citizen and on society in general that must concern us most.

The jurors and alternates are ordinary citizens summoned to perform a duty for the community. This is a great sacrifice since jurors and alternates are not compensated at even a small fraction of the level of compensation of professionals involved in the criminal justice system—such as lawyers and expert witnesses. Their lives are disrupted and their private matters are often exposed to the public. In addition, they have less freedom of action than any of the other participants in the trial—except possibly the defendant in the case. The exuberant media coverage that tends to legitimize mere rumors and to give full faith and value to unsubstantiated, coarse racial allegations has caused the public to become increasingly cynical and polarized. This phenomenon is reflected in the polls of black and white

Americans, conducted mostly by media, that show dangerously diverging opinion on the guilt or innocence of O.J. Simpson.

Because of apprehension in both the black and white communities across the country about the racial implications of the Simpson case, I visited the trial—accompanied by Celes King, CORE's California state chairman, and by George Holmes, my deputy at CORE's national headquarters—to talk with the judge and the attorneys in the case. I pleaded with them—Judge Lance Ito, Johnnie Cochran, Robert Shapiro, Marcia Clark, and Chris Darden—to do everything in their power to keep out or at least to minimize racial input in the trial. Predictably all parties agreed, even if the behavior of some of them, before or after, did not conform to their pronouncement.

When Jeanette Harris, one of the former jurors, was dismissed by Judge Ito, a media feeding frenzy was created when she alleged that racial tensions existed among the sequestered jurors and with the sheriff deputies assigned to guard them. Judge Ito apparently reacted precipitately to her allegations by removing the deputies from that assignment, but most of the remaining jurors and alternates—both black and white—responded with a dramatic show of support for the maligned deputies. It was clear that Ms. Harris did not represent the views of a significant number of other jurors.

I had hoped that a more neutral, objective description of events and the feelings among the jurors and alternates could be made available to the public. That neutral, objective sketch has been supplied by Michael Knox, a former member of the jury. Mike Knox is a breath of fresh air in a post–Rodney King environment increasingly polluted with explicit and implicit racism (real or imagined). Courageously, he has attempted to document a process that instinctively he suspected would have a profound and dramatic impact on America.

Increasing racism is a paradox in today's America. America has won one of the great social/political revolutions in the history of humankind, and it was achieved in a relatively short time and by relatively peaceful means. The civil rights movement of the

1950s and 1960s changed America profoundly, and that cannot be denied. Overt racism that operated with legal sanctions has been contained, and covert racism that operated with social sanctions has been exposed. On the other hand, despite the great success of the civil rights movement and its liberating effects—on blacks, whites, Hispanics, Asians, and Native Americans—there seems to be an increasing preoccupation with racial issues. All revolutions, whether peaceful or violent, have unfortunate by-products. This phenomenon—racial hypersensitivity—is a negative by-product of this revolution.

The civil rights revolution, while awakening America to racial injustice, has oversensitized it to race. A reflexive syndrome relating to race affects the behavior of all Americans—especially blacks and whites. It has reached the level of an addiction. Americans, while trying to do the right thing, have become a nation of race-addicted junkies. Both blacks and whites are addicted psychologically to race, although their addictions are expressed differently. In most situations involving blacks and whites, the initial response is reflexively racial: blacks in general react with a twinge of paranoia; whites react with a pang of a guilt complex.

Americans (especially blacks and whites) have institutionalized these reflexive racial reactions into a politically correct way of responding and dealing with each other. Many whites expect and accept that blacks would be a little paranoid about white racism. On the other hand, many blacks expect whites to demur and to have a guilt complex about past and present racism. Even worse, a veritable reign of intellectual terror is developing in black America to enforce this politically correct way of relating to racial matters. Blacks are expected to react as a monolith!

Mike Knox is challenging this forced, expected conformity to a monolithic racial judgement. He has challenged the popular and accepted falsehoods usually told about racial matters. He has broken the conspiracy of silence imposed on the black community—by the black community. Finally, unlike most jurors, he has made a clarion call for change in the dehumanizing conditions that jurors must endure during sequestration. A determined attempt was made by the criminal justice system of California to mute Mike Knox's clarion call for reform and reason. Knox and his publisher Dove Books courageously resisted this infringement on their First Amendment rights. A federal district court ruled against the California justice system, upholding Mike Knox's and Dove Books' right to publish.

Michael Knox is not a black leader or a politician. He is a regular American who has lived a unique experience. He has no axe to grind, no special interest to pursue. He is the voice of America's silent majority—he is particularly the voice of the silenced black majority.

The Private Diary
of an O.J. Juror

1 ⚖️ The Jury Room

MARCH 1, 1995

9:35 A.M.

"Juror 620!"

My skin jumped.

Goddam, I hated being a number . . . getting a nervous twitch every time I heard "620!" called out suddenly, sharply, like a summons to Judgment Day with a big voice booming: "You're just a number, sinner . . . and your number is UP!"

The eyes of my fellow jurors swept over me, then dropped as I glanced around nervously like a man who wanted someone to tell him it was all just a mistake. My stomach lurched and I suddenly felt queasy. To this day, I don't know if I suspected what was coming, but I'd had premonitions, some bad dreams. I was jumpy all the time now. Powerful people had laid the evil eye on me, and one of them had hurt me bad already.

"Juror Number 620! Judge Ito wants to see you in his chambers."

Deirdre Robertson, Judge Lance A. Ito's assistant, stood in the doorway of the ninth floor jury room, smiling expectantly. As my eyes met hers, she made the tiniest shrug, as if to say, "Sorry, time to face the music."

I rose from my chair. All of us, every juror, knew what it meant to be summoned to Judge Ito's chambers. We'd seen it happen before . . . Juror Number 96, Juror Number 112, and Juror Number 37. Now Juror Number 620 might just be slated to join the roll call of nameless numbers who'd never again sit in the jury box to deliberate on the guilt or innocence of O.J. Simpson.

I walked toward Deirdre Robertson, a pleasant-looking African-American woman in her thirties. I cleared my throat and said, "Can you give me a moment to go to the men's room?" She said, "Of course," and stepped aside. I was back a few minutes later, and as I followed her down the hall to Judge Ito's chambers, my mind was racing. What did the judge want? What had I done? I had a strong feeling it had something to do with the jury's recent weekend field trip to Brentwood. What a weird experience that had been. Finally, we'd seen the very spot where Nicole Brown Simpson and Ronald Lyle Goldman had been murdered, then toured O.J.'s Rockingham estate.

As I thought back on that day, images of the incredible media circus sprang up—the news helicopters, the mobs of reporters and what seemed like hundreds of policemen riding in black-and-whites, or on motorcycles. And I remembered a face that glared at me fiercely, angrily . . . the face of prosecutor Christopher Darden.

Darden had been standing in the living room of Nicole's condominium as I walked in the door with a group of jurors. Right next to him was Johnnie Cochran. I remember Cochran looking at me quizzically, then shifting his glance away. But Darden's eyes locked onto mine, glowering. He didn't like what he was seeing, but I didn't know why—and I wouldn't find out until much later. At the time I remember thinking, Darden and Johnnie Cochran act like they hate each other in the courtroom, so why do they look all buddy-buddy now?

As Deirdre and I walked down the hall, courtroom workers passed by, nodding at her and looking curiously at me. The word would be all over the building in five minutes: "Something's up with Juror Number 620!" I remember turning to Deirdre and asking, "So what's the judge want?" She just shrugged. A clerk of the court knows a lot of secrets, and knows how to keep them.

My mind wouldn't stop trying to figure out why Judge Ito wanted me. I was like a kid called to the principal's office. Then something triggered my memory. I thought back to an incident that had occurred at O.J.'s Rockingham estate the day of the field trip. I had thought it was fairly minor at the time, but maybe it was more crucial than I'd realized. It began when our vans rolled up to O.J.'s estate. We stood up and were already filing out when Judge Ito suddenly appeared.

He got on the bus, actually bucking the line headed the other way and called out something like: "Jurors, give me your attention, please. I want to warn you that when you enter Mr. Simpson's house, I don't want you looking at the photographs on the wall or throughout the house. You'll see that there are a lot of photos, but I don't want you stopping to look at them closely. Is that clear?"

Everybody mumbled, "Yes, Judge . . . Yes, sir," as we pushed our way out into the sunshine. What a treat to be away from the courtroom and our hotel. I stepped out of the van eagerly. You just can't imagine what a treat it was for all the jurors to be out in the fresh air. It was a gorgeous California day, and we could enjoy it more here at Rockingham because we weren't looking at the murder site.

O.J.'s estate wasn't quite as large and imposing as I'd imagined it. But it was no shack, either. Some of the other black jurors and I exchanged looks, and I knew we were all thinking the same thing: This was the home of a black man who'd grabbed his piece of the American Dream.

We toured the house in groups. Once inside, I momentarily forgot Judge Ito's warning that jurors should not look at any of the photographs. I walked in the door and was riveted immediately by the immense wall displays of framed photos showing O.J. with the rich and famous . . . with family and friends . . . in his football days. There were photos all over that house. As I stared at them, one of the female jurors I'd grown friendly with caught my eye and glared, warning me off.

Now, as Deirdre Robertson and I approached Judge Ito's chambers, I thought, Man, it couldn't be that! Do they think I couldn't make a fair judgment of O.J. just because I'd looked at a couple of pictures? I can't believe he'd throw me off the jury for that!

I'd know soon enough. Deirdre stepped ahead of me as we approached the judge's chambers. She knocked, then opened the door and stepped aside, motioning me in. Suddenly, I felt like I was on trial. I don't mind admitting that I felt apprehensive, and still slightly nauseous, as I walked into the room and saw some of the most famous faces in America staring back at me—Marcia Clark, Chris Darden, Robert Shapiro, Johnnie Cochran, and Judge Ito. Man, oh man . . . this looked heavy.

I thought of the four jurors who had been ordered off the jury. Was I next? Two of those jurors I'd never gotten to know; they were gone so early on in the trial. But the other, Jeanette Harris . . . now there was a woman I'd never forget. No one involved in the O.J. trial would ever forget Jeanette.

2 ⚖

Jeanette: "Juror Furor"

APRIL 1995

Michael Knox, Juror Number 620 until he'd been thrown off the jury by Judge Ito on March 1, 1995, sat in the living room of his modest home in Long Beach watching in astonishment as Juror Number 309, Jeanette Harris, revealed for the first time in a TV interview that the O.J. jury was about to explode.

"Beverly," he called out. "Come in here . . . you won't believe this."

His wife came in from outside, carrying Johnnie, the fourteen-month-old foster baby they hoped to adopt. Johnnie always got a lot of attention when he went outside with his

African-American foster mother. It's not just that he was adorable; he was white, with blond hair and blue eyes.

"Who's that?" Beverly asked as she sat down and looked at the TV screen.

"You remember her. Jeanette Harris. You saw her on visiting days."

"Oh, right. She's the one who never talked much."

"Yeah, well, she sure is talking now."

On the Channel 9 news, anchorwoman Pat Harvey was in the middle of an interview with Jeanette Harris. The thirty-eight-year-old juror had been bounced on April 5, 1995, after Judge Ito learned that she had accused her husband of beating her in 1988, even though she'd denied any connection with domestic violence in her jury questionnaire. Now Jeanette Harris, wearing the smug look of a woman ready to settle some scores, had the world waiting to hear her tell all on TV— and she was about to lob a bombshell right to Judge Ito's lap.

After expressing her contempt for the prosecution and Detective Mark Fuhrman—

and dismissing the testimony of Nicole's sister Denise Brown as "acting"—Harris told anchor Pat Harvey, an African-American journalist, that she didn't find the Los Angeles Police Department to be credible. Then she lashed out at the sheriff's deputies who guarded the jurors around the clock.

HARRIS: "There are racial problems, and the deputies, not to bad-mouth the sheriff's department . . . but some of them are promoting [racial problems] . . . . During the whole time we were being selected, they kept saying 'This is not a racial case. Don't think of race.' And when we were locked up, race was always an issue that you were not supposed to think about. But there is a problem with the ethnic breakup of the group."

HARVEY: "O.K., so within the jurors themselves there were racial problems. Is that what you are saying?"

HARRIS: "Yes, there are racial problems. You know, if they had a different attitude— like I explained to the sergeant, because I was really concerned about that—that I feel they should be more professional. They're not being—some of them are not being very professional and it's going to come across. It has to. It has to. Because these are people, and it's a wonderful thing to say, 'You know, you are at court, and when you make your decision, make your decision based on that.' That's easy to say. But it's not that easy to do. And those things cross your mind while you are sitting there."

HARVEY: "Do you think that the fact that the majority of the jury is black makes a difference on how you will decide this case? Or can you decide on the basis of the evidence alone? There have been reports from a lot of people that because it is a majority black jury, this jury will not convict O.J. Simpson."

HARRIS: "Well, I wouldn't just say because a person is black that they would feel that he is not guilty, no. I just—in my mind, I can think of a couple of jurors—that's just my opinion—that probably would say, 'Oh, yeah, he's guilty' sitting there right now on the jury. But no, it's not, just a fact that he's an African-American man, and we're African Americans, that we're gonna say 'not guilty.' No."

HARVEY: "So you think he can get a fair trial?"

HARRIS: "I wouldn't say I think he can get a fair trial. I don't see a fair trial. From day one, I didn't see it being a fair trial."

Michael Knox turned away from the TV screen and shook his head in disbelief. "Oh man, she has opened a can of worms now."

"You mean because she says O.J. can't get a fair trial?" his wife asked.

"No, Beverly, it's because she's telling the world that there's bad racial tension on the jury. And she's calling the white deputies racists. What she's trying to say is that O.J. won't get a fair trial because the race thing is putting pressure on everybody. I'm telling you right now, Beverly, the courtroom is going to go nuts tomorrow. Judge Ito's going to call for a big investigation."

"Is she right, Michael?"

"She's right when she says there are racists on that jury. But she's wrong when she says it's the white deputies."

"What do you mean, Michael? Who—"

"Wait. Wait, let me hear this, baby."

On the screen, Jeanette Harris was saying, "The pressure is too great on that jury. To be perfectly honest, I see a hung jury."

Michael Knox whistled in amazement. "Oh man, this woman is starting BIG trouble."

On the TV screen, Jeanette Harris launched into a rambling, somewhat confused rap about how white jurors would be afraid to vote O.J. "not guilty" because once back in their neighborhoods they'd be condemned by other whites—and that African-American jurors who felt O.J. was guilty would be afraid to vote honestly because they'd dread explaining their decision to family and friends.

Then Jeanette Harris dropped her next bombshell. She implied that despite Judge Ito's orders, jurors were discussing the case.

Michael Knox leaned back in his chair

and looked at his wife with raised eyebrows. "Beverly, there's going to be hell to pay. You mark my words. I've seen Jeanette Harris operate, and she's a woman who just loves to manipulate people. What you just saw was her practically begging Judge Ito to call her back into his chambers and let her spill her guts.

"That woman's looking to make a few people's lives miserable. And she's going to do it, Beverly. Mark my words."

In the days to come, the firestorm that the media had dubbed "Juror Furor" raged out of control . . . even faster and more furiously than Michael Knox could have guessed. Suddenly, Americans caught up in O.J. Mania had a new legal word to chew on: Mistrial!

New York Daily News, **Friday, April 14, 1995—** An ousted O.J. Simpson case juror painted her most shocking picture yet of a segregated panel—a jury divided by racial tension and rocked by violent clashes.

"You know, this is not just little trivial things

that come off the top of my head," Jeanette Harris told Judge Ito in sworn testimony. "There were literally racial problems," added the thirty-eight-year-old African American, according to an explosive transcript released yesterday.

Harris's latest batch of bombshells was dropped in a meeting Wednesday night with Ito, who is probing the panel amid talk of a mistrial over the racially torn jury. The employment counselor last week became the sixth juror bounced from the case after it was revealed she had lied about her domestic violence history—leading some to question her credibility.

New York Post, Friday, April 14, 1995—Shocking new racial bombshells exploded at the O.J. Simpson trial yesterday as an ousted juror told of fear and loathing among the sequestered panelists.

Not only did black and white jurors exercise in separate gyms, but a white juror and Hispanic juror ganged up to wallop a black juror on the head, according to transcripts released yesterday.

Former juror Jeanette Harris, in a scathing

review of her time on the O.J. jury, told Judge Lance Ito that twenty-four-hour sequestration, improper behavior by sheriff's deputies, and the ill tempers of some jurors turned the experience into a living hell.

Things became so intense that there is "bad blood" between certain jurors that can never be reversed, she said.

New York Newsday, Friday, April 14, 1995—A dismissed O.J. Simpson juror has told Superior Court Judge Lance Ito that the jury is so racially divided that they use separate gyms and movie rooms, that sheriff's deputies show favoritism toward whites, and that the atmosphere is like a prison's, with room searches and jurors wondering who next will be missing from their number.

3

⚖️

Judge Ito's Chambers

MARCH 1, 1995

9:45 A.M.

A court reporter sat clicking away at her transcriber as Judge Ito questioned me in his chambers. Somewhere in the court records are the exact words, but it went something like this: "Mr. Knox, we have received a report that you made a bet at your place of work with one of your fellow employees that Mr. Simpson would walk. Is this true, Mr. Knox?"

It was so unexpected, it took me a few seconds to absorb what he had said. Then I looked him right in the eye and said, "No, Judge. I never made a bet with anybody."

Judge Ito sat there in shirt sleeves, his judicial robe hanging from a clothes tree beside his desk. He returned my gaze, not unkindly, but like a man who had some business to do.

"We are told, Mr. Knox, that you bet a week's salary that O.J. Simpson would walk out of this courtroom a free man. I'm asking you again, did you make any such bet?"

When I heard that, I almost laughed out loud. A wave of frustration hit me. This was so weird, so unreal. I said something like, "Judge, I have a family to support. There is no way I would bet a week's salary on anything. Who's telling you this stuff?"

Judge Ito sat silently behind his desk, looking at me with measuring eyes. I turned slightly in my chair. Sitting on a sofa beside me, Johnnie Cochran and Robert Shapiro were impassive, and Chris Darden wasn't glaring at me this time. But Marcia Clark stared at me with distinct unfriendliness. Now what the hell?, I wondered.

Behind the attorneys stood two tall, heavily built black men, who hadn't moved since I came into the room. Police detectives,

I thought, or some kind of investigators or marshals. Now I believe they were the two sheriff's detectives assigned to help the judge investigate jurors. I turned back to Judge Ito. He still sat silently, framed by tall bookcases of law volumes behind him. After a moment, he nodded, almost like he'd decided that he believed my answer. Or like he had bigger fish to fry.

"O.K., Mr. Knox. Let me move on to something that I find quite serious. On the questionnaire that you filled out before you were impaneled on this jury, you noted that you had two arrests, one involving petty theft and one on a firearms charge. . . ."

I tensed. Now I knew what was coming before he uttered another word. Inside my head, the little voice that keeps score until the day we die cursed at me, "Man, what a damn fool you are!"

Judge Ito continued. "The third charge that you failed to note is far more serious, Mr. Knox. The charge is kidnapping."

The judge's eyes bored right into my soul. I felt all the air go out of me. I couldn't meet his eyes. How the hell had I been stupid

4 ⚖
Michael Knox:
Bio

The gun charge. Man, that was pure bull-shit. It happened in San Diego back in 1982. I was stuck in slow-and-go traffic coming out of the Jack Murphy Stadium parking lot. It was a hot day, the Chargers had lost to the Kansas City Chiefs and I was wondering if the kid I'd left in charge of the record shop I owned back then had made a few sales while I'd been sitting on my ass out in the bleachers. In the backseat of the car, my then-wife Dovie and her sister were chatting away.

Traffic finally started to move steadily, and I looked forward to picking up speed and getting across the city to my favorite bar. Then everything slowed to a crawl again. In a few minutes, I saw why. There was a fight going on up ahead. Everybody was slowing down to gawk at it. Man, I thought, haven't these people ever seen a fight before?

I blew my horn angrily. A white couple, an older man and his wife, swung around in their seats and looked back at me. Right away they got that funny look on their faces that black men know so well. It said, Uh, oh, that's a mean-looking black guy. Let's haul ass. They hauled ass. Moments later, I came up on the fight. And naturally, I slowed down, even though I'd just been cursing at everybody else for doing it. I laughed. What the hell, I'm only human.

As I passed by the brawl I slowed down. Two huge, leather-clad white bikers were beating on an older black man. The guy was in real bad trouble. The bikers had him down on the asphalt, kicking him like they didn't mean to stop. Then one of them pulled a knife and put it against the black man's throat. My heart froze. I didn't know that poor man from Adam, but all of a sudden I just identified with him. He was a brother—

and a dead brother if somebody didn't help him.

By now, a crowd of pedestrians and people who'd gotten out of their cars had gathered around. Not to help. Hell no! They just wanted to gawk. Then I saw one of the bikers gesture impatiently at the guy who was holding the knife at the black man's throat. Goddam, he's gonna cut him for real, I thought.

In that split second, I made a decision that still makes me shudder today. I'm no hero, but I slammed on my brakes and almost without thinking reached into the glove compartment for the gun I usually kept in the cash drawer at my record store. Sometimes when I had a lot of cash to take home for deposit at the bank the next day, I'd take the gun along. It was an old piece my dad had given me. I'd never even used it.

I threw open the car door. I heard my wife and sister-in-law screaming, "Michael, come back. . . . Are you crazy?" As I ran across the parking lot I brandished the gun at the crowd, forcing them to pull back. I didn't know if the bikers had pals in the crowd, so I figured I'd just threaten everybody. They backed off fast. Then I leveled the gun at the biker holding the knife to my brother's throat.

"Back off, motherfucker!" I screamed. "Back off now or I'll blow your ass wide open."

These were some cold sons of bitches. The guy with the knife stared at me, not moving or acting scared, just making this nasty little smile. The other guy looked cool, like I'd asked him what time it was. They showed no fear and that was scary. Didn't these bastards see the gun in my hand?

Then they slowly backed off. The guy with the knife gestured with his chin at my gun and said, "You've got the power, man." The two of them, huge guys, both about six foot three, turned their backs and walked away, all chains and leather. They got into a grungy-looking Datsun 240Z sports car. Before they could take off, a gang of young black guys suddenly ran out of the crowd and started rocking the car, trying to tip it over before the bikers could take off. Where had these heroes been when I was standing out there alone? Then I heard one of the black kids scream, "Look out, man . . . he almost cut me!" There was a squeal of tires and the bikers took off, barreling right through the crowd as people yelled and scattered.

I turned to help the black victim, who was in bad shape. Those assholes had really nailed him. He was struggling, trying to get up. There was blood all over him, spraying, bubbling out of his mouth every time he tried to breathe.

"Just take it easy, man. You could be hurt bad inside," I told him.

I started yelling at cars passing by to call an ambulance. What I didn't know was that there was a off-duty San Diego plainclothes cop in the crowd. He'd been attending the game and had come running up to check out the commotion. He'd arrived just in time to see me waving a gun around—and a bloody victim on the ground. I didn't know it, but he was already radioing for an ambulance and police backup. By that time, other people were attending to the man on the ground. My wife was yelling at me to come back, and I told him I had to move my car. He thanked

27

me and told me to take off. He managed to tell me his name, Harold Tolson, and asked me to look him up at a store he owned.

I got back in my car and started out of the parking lot. Then I heard sirens and saw flashing lights up ahead. The line of cars slowed down again, and I thought, now what? We inched forward, stop and go. Then Dovie, who'd stepped out of the car at one point to see what was going on, said, "Oh my God! The cops are doing a roadblock. They're searching cars." Oh, man! My first thought was the gun. I had to hide it. I wasn't too worried because I didn't think anyone in the crowd would point me out to the cops. I didn't think those bikers had any friends in the crowd. I hoped not, anyway. I handed Dovie the gun and told her to hide it in one of my drum cases that were in the backseat. Moments later, it was our turn to be searched. As my car pulled up to where the cops were waiting, my heart sank. Some white guy in plainclothes with a badge pinned to his shirt was pointing me out to the uniformed cops, saying, "That's him!"

Suddenly I had guns in my face. The

cops yanked me out of the car and slammed me up against a wall, hard. I kept yelling that I hadn't done anything. They just bounced me into the wall again until I shut up. Then one of them yelled, "Here's the gun!"

By this time I was handcuffed. They frog-marched me over to a black-and-white and shoved me in. As the uniformed cops got in the car, I tried to explain again what had happened, but suddenly realized it was no use. These were white cops who'd been told by another white cop that he'd seen a black man waving a gun. He hadn't seen the bikers, and by the time this mess was straightened out, I was guaranteed at least one night in jail—if I was lucky!

Man, I was angry. There was no reason for this to be happening. But I knew it was useless to argue with the cops. All that would get me was a billy club upside the head, or worse. Better to wait until I got downtown. I knew this would get straightened out. There was no way they could hold me on this bull-shit charge.

I just hoped my name wouldn't get in the newspapers. I sure didn't want to embarrass my family. Not that they'd be totally shocked. I'd always been the black sheep. That's right, even in black families we call it "the black sheep." Oh, man! Dad wasn't going to like this. He could be as hard-headed as these cops if he thought you'd messed up.

My father ran a tight ship. He'd spent his entire career in the U.S. Navy, what they call a "lifer." He was a stern, religious man with a strong sense of duty. Life for a black man in the U.S. Navy in his day was tough. You knew you'd never rise very high. Yet if you toed the line, if you were a spit-shine sailor, you could get some respect. But you always had to know your place.

As navy brats, my two brothers and three sisters and I grew up in ports from Jacksonville, Florida, to San Diego, California. Dad was captain of our household ship but he counted on first mate Mom to carry out his orders of the day. It worked pretty well. Sure, we moved around a lot and were constantly saying good-bye to school friends. But we learned how to be confident in strange situations. And despite the segregation in the navy, we were constantly thrown together with white people, so we learned how to get along in both worlds.

Mom and Dad insisted we do our schoolwork, attend church with them every Sunday, and keep ourselves clean and neat. We sure weren't rich, but we never went hungry. Our parents loved us and protected us. And they were great believers in putting your best foot forward and facing life unafraid. They always told us not to judge people by their religion or the color of their skin. "There are bad white people," Dad used to say. "But there are bad black people, too. A good man is a good man, and that's all that should count."

We were a handful, like any kids, but Mom and Dad must have done something right. Nearly all my brothers and sisters have college degrees. Me, I attended the College of Life and ended up playing drums in pickup bands around San Diego. It's no secret that a musician's life can be pretty flaky. Yet I've known many who were solid family men, who went straight home after every gig

31

and never drank, did drugs, or chased women. In my case, it took a lot of the latter before I finally became the former.

Today I am very happily married to my lovely wife, Beverly, and have four foster children, two adopted children, and one natural child. I work at Federal Express and have a moonlighting job as a security guard. Playing drums is just a hobby, although I love to sit in and jam with buddies who are still working musicians.

Trouble? I've had my share, but I sure wasn't a criminal. I've never run with the gangs. My only other run-in with the law was one that I deserved—I stole a motorcycle battery and was charged with petty theft, a misdemeanor.

This time, sitting in that police cruiser and on my way to jail, I knew I was in more serious trouble. A gun possession charge was no joke. But I knew I'd walk away from it—and that's just what happened. My grandmother used to attend the same church as a man who, in those days, was the only black sergeant in the San Diego Police Department. When Dovie told her I'd been arrested,

Grandma contacted Sergeant Johnny Williams. He made a phone call to the station house and vouched for me. A few hours later I was released. The charge was dropped and I never carried a gun again.

I'd never had any trouble admitting to those two run-ins with the law. I wasn't proud of them. The petty theft was the kind of stupid thing you do when you're young. And the gun possession charge was nothing very serious. But the kidnapping—that one made me ashamed. It sounds like such a violent, despicable crime. I hated the word.

Kidnapping.

The few times I've admitted it to anyone I've been shamed by the shocked, incredulous look in their eyes.

Kidnapping.

The word sickened me. And that's why I couldn't put it down on the O.J. jury questionnaire. I wouldn't have lied or tried to cover it up if the lawyers had asked me about it during the voir dire questioning. But I just couldn't write down that hateful word without any explanation. I wouldn't have had any problem telling somebody about it, explaining that what had actually happened didn't deserve to be called "kidnapping"—by any reasonable person—even though the law says that's the legal description of the crime I'd been accused of committing.

Let me tell you how it went down: I had a girlfriend back in the early 1980s, a hot-looking black woman who worked as a stripper. Her name was Clare. We were crazy about each other. She used to tell me, "Baby, you are the most loving man I've ever met. I just can't get enough of you." And I'd tell her, "You're my perfect woman. You drive me crazy and I'll never leave you." It was all heat and passion, and the inevitable by-product of our red-hot affair was jealousy. It's tough to handle when your girlfriend is a stripper who's seen naked by hundreds of men every night. We didn't fight a lot, but it was bammin' slammin' when it happened.

One day, we got into a really nasty quarrel because I found out Clare had been talking on the phone to an old boyfriend. She had a day job as a secretary, and when it was time for her to go to work, she flounced out of the house, cursing me.

"I'll talk to anybody I goddam please," she screamed.

I sat there stewing and drinking, and stewing some more. Then I headed over to where Clare worked. When she saw me there, all hell broke loose. We started screaming and shoving each other and finally ended up in the parking lot. Suddenly, in the heat of my rage, I grabbed Clare, shoved her into my car, and drove off with her.

A crowd of people had seen us fighting, and I worried that somebody might call the cops. But I needn't have worried about a stranger turning me in; Clare did that herself. After I had driven her back home, I kept sweet-talking her and trying to make up. But she had a strange look in her eye, that "hell hath no fury" look. She was going to get back at me. And that's just what she did. About an hour later, the police came and arrested me. When I heard the charge was kidnapping, I almost fainted. The cops laughed and said that if they'd picked me up for fighting at the house, the charge would have been domestic abuse. But because I had shoved her in the car while she was out in public, or "imprisoned" her, I was charged with "kidnapping." Unbelievable!

The whole thing came to nothing. I spent a few hours in jail. Then I called Clare and begged her to get me out. She dropped the charges and that night we were making passionate love in our own bed. It was just one of those incidents that doesn't seem like much at the time—but sounds real bad years later when you have to explain it. And here's the real reason I didn't figure I had to write down that old charge on the jury question- naire: The cops had told me that the records were sealed.

I'd just learned a new point of law: You can't seal anything from a judge.

5

Judge Ito's Chambers

MARCH 1, 1995

9:50 A.M.

Judge Ito's question rang in my ears. "Mr. Knox, why did you fail to note that you had been arrested for kidnapping on your questionnaire?" I shook my head and tried to explain. Judge Ito listened intently. I finished by saying, "Judge, we were making love that night like nothing had ever happened and my girlfriend kept saying how happy she was that she had her man back."

The minute I said that, Marcia Clark, who'd been glaring at me ever since I'd walked into the room made a snorting noise and rolled her eyes in what appeared to be

37

total disgust. She sort of threw up her hands and dropped some papers on the floor. Wow! I don't know what her problem was, but I guess she was thinking something like, what kind of a macho jerk is this guy?!

As I recall, Judge Ito didn't say a word about my story. He just told me to leave and wait outside until he made his decision on whether or not I'd continue to sit in the jury box of the most notorious celebrity murder trial of the century.

Judge Ito's assistant escorted me back to the ninth floor jury room. Everyone stopped talking when I walked inside and sat down. My insides were churning. This time it wasn't butterflies; it was rage. I looked around the jury room. It was cramped, uncomfortable, unlike the spacious area on the eleventh floor where we ate our meals during court sessions. Here we sat practically on top of one another. It was almost impossible to look around without meeting someone else's eyes. But as I glanced at my fellow jurors, every eye managed to avoid mine. Somehow, that angered me even more.

Here I sat, under the gun, and they all knew it. No one had any illusions about the meaning of a summons to Judge Ito's chambers. My fellow jurors knew that if I'd been called in for something minor, and had managed to answer Judge Ito's questions satisfactorily, I would have said something. They sensed I was waiting to be summoned again, to be told my fate. Yet no one spoke or acknowledged me by so much as a glance.

I thought, I've been with these people, locked away in forced intimacy for nearly two months, yet not one of them is willing to speak to me or even smile in sympathy.

I looked at each one, my anger growing. How well I'd come to know these people, their personalities. My eyes swept the room again. I looked at each of them: the Manipulator; the Bully; the Health Nut; the Timid Beauty; the Lesbian; the Bitter Old Man; Mister Bad Breath; the Sexpot . . .

Nothing can ever erase the bitterness I felt at that moment. I thought, How had this all gone so very wrong? I had joined these people with a sense of excitement at being included in a history-making case that had the eyes of America, even the world, riveted upon us. But beyond that excitement, I had begun to feel a sense of commitment, of duty, of an obligation to do the right thing. I remember how, after the initial thrill of being chosen for the O.J. Simpson jury had worn off, I had started to think of the tremendous responsibility we all had. A man's life was at stake. We had to do right by O.J. Simpson; yet the families of two innocent people who had been brutally murdered cried out for justice. Somebody had to speak for them.

From the time of the murders until we were impaneled as a jury, all twenty-four of us—and probably all Americans—had experienced shock and disbelief as one of the nation's best-known celebrities had been accused of a heinous crime. Now America was polarized. The question of O.J.'s guilt or innocence raged in constant argument among millions of people.

This was no clear-cut case. I'm just a normal guy, and I found it incredibly difficult to follow the legal twists and turns. Like most folks, I followed the case on TV and watched countless discussions among lawyers, journalists, talk show hosts, experts, and so-called "experts." Over and over, I heard it said that this case was a classic "whodunit." There were no eyewitnesses, no murder weapon. But there was a trail of blood leading from the murder scene into O.J.'s Bronco and, allegedly, even into his bedroom. It was a circumstantial case. Motive, means, and opportunity had to be proven beyond a reasonable doubt; a tough challenge for the prosecution, an awesome responsibility for the jury.

I'd been prepared, even eager. And so, at first, was the majority of my fellow jurors. But almost from the start, deep-rooted tensions ripped us apart.

Now, sitting there in that jury room, waiting for Judge Ito's decision, anger and bitterness welled up again. Damn, I thought, how the hell had the O.J. Simpson case turned into my personal nightmare? Here I sat, waiting to be thrown off one of the most high-profile juries in history—and facing the threat of public humiliation when the reason for my dismissal was revealed. And if you think that's trouble . . . you ain't heard nothin' yet.

From the very moment it became known that I was headed for the O.J. jury, I had endured harassment and vicious racism from co-workers at Federal Express. I had worked there for eight years. But once I was named as an O.J. jury candidate, I was suddenly demoted.

I didn't know it then, but there'd be more bad news in the days to come. I'd be falsely labeled a wife beater in the pages of the *Los Angeles Times*. And I'd be accused of getting a female juror pregnant. In just a few short months, my life had been snatched up by a whirlwind, and I still had no idea where I'd come down. My mind reeled back to the beginning, that same beginning all America had shared . . . The Chase!

6 ⚖️
The Chase

JUNE 16, 1994

6:10 P.M.

"O.J.'s on the run in his white Bronco."

Moments before, I'd hopped out of my red-white-and-blue Federal Express van to drop off a package for one of my regular customers. When the guy came to the door, he was so excited he didn't even reach for his package. He started babbling that O.J. Simpson, who'd suddenly disappeared earlier that day after promising to turn himself in to the police, had been spotted.

"Come on in, you've got to see this," said the guy, waving me inside where his TV was blaring.

"Look, the cops are following that white Bronco. They think O.J.'s inside and Al Cowlings [A.C.] is driving. They think O.J. might have a gun. It's unbelievable."

I'll never forget the look on that man's face—he was really excited. Looking back on it now, I realized that The Chase, as a moment in history, was not unlike the JFK assassination: If you'd experienced it, you always remembered exactly where you were at the moment you heard about it.

I stayed at that man's house for about ten minutes, watching the eerie, slow-moving cavalcade of police cruisers following O.J. with their lights flashing. The scene filled me with dread. O.J. was going to die. I was sure of it. In talks I had later with friends, neighbors, and co-workers—both black and white—I learned that almost everyone had experienced a sense of foreboding; but not for the same reasons.

Most white people, like my customer, feared O.J. would commit suicide. But black people, myself included, had believed that O.J. would be executed during The Chase by the Los Angles Police Department. It's tough to explain this black paranoia to a white person who's been taught since birth that policemen are your friends, always there to protect and to serve. But for any black male who's grown up through years of systematic and officially condoned racism by LAPD cops, it's a slam dunk equation: Black male running from white cops equals certain death! Unless you're lucky enough to get off with a beating.

There's no doubt—none!—that had Daryl Gates still been police chief of Los Angeles, O.J. Simpson's life would have ended in a hail of police bullets. It's only because the riot-torn city had finally hired a black man, Police Chief Willie Williams, that O.J. is alive today. Under Daryl Gates, racist cops with itchy trigger fingers would know they'd get away with nothing more than a wrist slapping if they shot a black man—as long as they didn't put every bullet hole through his back! But the cops riding The Chase in their black-and-whites that day knew that the world was watching. The prospect of facing a black police chief and explaining away a dead black celebrity had a numbing effect on the trigger fingers of racist cops that day—if there were any.

Fair is fair, and there are lots of good cops in the LAPD. But if you're not black, and you think I'm being overly paranoid, ask a black friend. Better yet, if you've got a pal who's a white police officer, ask him if it's true that many police forces harbor a small, hard-core group of racist cops who would kill a black man with little or no provocation.

I hold down a second job as a security guard to support my wife, children, grand-children, and a dog. The night after The Chase, I stopped at a supermarket around midnight to pick up some soft drinks. I over-heard two Huntington Beach policemen talk-ing about O.J., and one of them said, "If I'd been in that chase, the taxpayers wouldn't be paying for a trial."

After I left my customer's house, I con-tinued along my route and picked up a prog-ress report at each stop. Everybody was watching The Chase. At first, it was far away in Orange County. But slowly it became ap-parent that O.J. was circling back towards the city.

"They think he's headed back to Brentwood," one customer told me as he absent-mindedly signed for his package.

I said, "That means he'll be coming down the 405 Freeway. Maybe I'll be seeing him."

"Yeah, you could run into him on your route."

"It's possible," I said. "We cover this area all the way over to Brentwood. A lot of drivers have delivered packages to O.J. and to Nicole at her condo over on Bundy."

It was true. In fact, it was well known that some of the couriers used to collect autographs from O.J. and other celebrities. They had to turn in the receipt slip the celebrity customer signed, of course, but they'd simply make copies for their private collections.

As I headed back out on my route that day, I started to see cars full of people headed toward the 405—obviously looking for O.J. You could easily spot the ones that were gripped by O.J. Mania! Their eyes darted around as they drove. It was like *Where's Waldo?* on wheels.

That was one crazy day. I picked up news from customers as I made stops along my route. I had no way of monitoring The Chase. Federal Express vans are equipped with dash units, a combination radio and computer. We can talk over the radio to the dispatcher and other drivers, but using the radio for chitchat about O.J. would have gotten me fired.

Finally, it was time to drive back to the station I worked out of and finish up my paperwork. Not many employees were still around, but a couple of them were watching The Chase on portable TV sets. I finished up my work and headed home.

My wife Beverly had the TV set on. Now O.J. and A.C.'s bizarre motorcade was headed for O.J.'s estate on Rockingham. I sat and watched, knowing I was part of a shared experience that was pulling in at least as many viewers as the L.A. riots. It was mind blowing. I remember my wife saying, "Do you think they'll kill him?"

"I can't believe he's made it this far," I said. "He's a fleeing fugitive with a gun, so it would be pretty easy to justify. But now that I think about it, O.J.'s got a better chance than most black men. He's probably got more white fans than black fans. Look at all those people lined up along the freeway. There's more whites and Hispanics standing out there cheering him than blacks. But if we still had Daryl Gates, O.J. would be history. They'd blow him away, no question. If O.J. makes it through this, he can thank Willie Williams."

My wife shook her head. "I just can't believe it! Here's a big football hero running down the freeway like a criminal. It's shocking. Seems like every time a black man raises himself up he gets knocked down, just like Mike Tyson and Michael Jackson. And Martin Luther King, Jr."

"You got that right, baby. But the guy who's really helping big time here is that reporter from KNX radio, the one who's been talking to Al Cowlings while they've been driving. If it wasn't for him keeping everybody up on what's going on in the Bronco, I think the cops would have gotten nervous by this time and done something to force the situation."

Finally, at around 8:00 P.M. The Chase

ended. My wife and I, along with the rest of L.A., went to bed. Downtown, O.J. lay alone in a tiny cell under a suicide watch, wrestling with his private demons. Would he sleep tonight? I wondered. O.J.'s nightmare was in full cry. Mine was just beginning.

7

Selection and Harassment

"Hey baby, look at this! I'll bet I'm gonna be an O.J. juror."

My wife Beverly had just walked in with her arms full of groceries. My four little foster kids, Johnnie, Darnell, Reynaldo, and Manuel, were yelling for her attention, along with my dog, Cookie.

"What's that you've got there?" she asked, cocking her chin at the paper I held in my hand. It was an official-looking document ordering me to report for jury duty. I read it to Beverly and she cut right to the chase.

"I don't hear anything in there about you being on an O.J. jury. It must be in some

51

kind of secret code I don't understand," she said with wide-eyed innocence.

"Beverly, don't be giving me the needle. You know damn well they're about to select the O.J. jury. What else could this be?"

"Well, I guess you've gotta go on down there and find out."

"What a drag, man." But inside I was secretly pleased. Ever since The Chase, I'd been fired up about the O.J. murder case. Now they were calling it "The Trial of the Century." O.J. Mania had America by the throat.

You went to work, you talked O.J. You met friends for dinner, you talked O.J. You went home, you turned on the TV and watched O.J. Every day at Federal Express, we'd argue the case during coffee breaks. It struck me again how many white people were O.J. fans. At first, none of them believed he'd done it. African Americans I talked to didn't seem as concerned about O.J.'s guilt or innocence. They were amazed that he appeared to be getting a fair shake.

As one black friend put it to me, "Man, if O.J. hadn't been a celebrity, he'd have been busted at least two or three days earlier. If that was you or me, or even some white guy who didn't have big connections, the bust would have gone down within a day, two days at the most. Hey, when somebody's old lady gets knifed and her husband shows up with a cut on his hand, you know the handcuffs are coming out. But the cops are walking real soft around O.J. That boy's practically white."

A few days later I reported to a state building on Commonwealth Avenue in downtown Los Angeles. Jury selection was going on in a huge room. It looked like a movie casting call. There were three hundred to four hundred people milling around, and if you stopped and listened intently, you heard one phrase buzzing around the room . . . "O.J. . . . O.J. . . . O.J. . . ." I struck up a conversation with an old guy there who looked like the spitting image of Fred Sanford, the TV character. He was a feisty old guy, an ex-musician who played accordion, so we hit it off right away.

"Man, all these people are just crazy, wanting to be on that O.J. jury," he said. "They think they're gonna end up in the history books. But they're gonna be sorry. O.J.'s got himself some fancy lawyers and a lot of money, so you know it's gonna be a long trial. Judge sticks their ass in some low-rent hotel, they're gonna wish they never heard of O.J."

I laughed. "How do we even know we're here to be on the O.J. jury? This could be for some other case or a bunch of cases."

Old Fred Sandford looked at me shrewdly. "Don't be running no game on me, Slick. You want to be diggin' on O.J. in that courtroom, just like everybody else. But that's alright, be cool. I ain't tellin' nobody." I laughed. Yeah, I told myself, I guess he's right.

The selection process was a drag. You got a questionnaire to fill out, then you'd go stand in one of several long lines out in the hallway. Eventually you'd end up in one of the smaller rooms outside the large room where you'd get interviewed. That's when I got my juror number—620. And that's when I first got to know Deirdre Robertson, Judge Ito's clerk. Deirdre had several assistants, or clerks of the court working with her. They'd ask us questions about our availability for jury service. Then we got handed another questionnaire asking how we'd feel about being sequestered. People took one look at that and started running to the telephones, calling their jobs and asking if they'd get paid during their time with the jury. That's when everybody became certain that we really were being looked at for the O.J. Simpson trial. I went home that night and told my wife, "It looks like O.J.!"

"Who's going to put food on the table while you're off doing jury duty?" she snapped. "On TV they're saying this trial could last six months. Who's gonna pay you?"

"Now Beverly, calm down. Federal Express pays the salary of anybody who serves jury duty, so that's no problem."

"Well, how about your second job as a security guard? Are they going to pay while you're not working?"

"No, but we'll be alright. They pay you some per diem money for jury duty. And my meals are free, so the grocery bill should be a lot lower."

"Who are you fooling? I hear on TV they only pay five dollars a day for a juror. So we're going to be making less money."

Now Beverly got upset. "I know what you want. You just want to serve on that O.J. jury," she said angrily.

Man, I must have been walking around with a big neon sign over my head saying, O.J. Juror Available. Later that night, we discussed it again. I admitted that I'd heard downtown that the O.J. jury would probably be sequestered. Beverly went nuts.

"I know you're lookin' for a vacation away from this house and our kids, but I didn't think you wanted to stop sleeping with me."

"Now, baby, you know that's not true . . ."

Well, you can fill in the rest of that.

Beverly got me to admit that some of us had asked the clerks about conjugal visits. We were told it was at the discretion of Judge Ito—but it was iffy.

The next day we were called back downtown again, this time to an even larger building on Temple Street. They hit us with a sixty-one-page questionnaire that had 294 questions to be answered.* We'd lost about fifty people from the first day, and we lost another fifty or sixty that second day. These people had been excused by the clerks when they insisted they just couldn't serve on a sequestered jury. And in a lot of cases, people complained of economic hardship because their companies refused to pay their salaries during jury duty. Just filling out that questionnaire took about four hours. Like I said, a real drag.

Over the next few days and weeks, the selection process moved slowly. As I survived each cut, I began to think I might really be selected. Finally, about two hundred of us—the survivors—reported to the courthouse,

---

*According to the *Los Angeles Daily Journal*'s Court Rules Service, California's leading law trade journal.

and attorneys on both sides started interviewing us.

So far, I'd kept all this quiet at work. The only person at Federal Express who knew that I was a juror candidate for the O.J. Simpson trial was my supervisor, a guy I'll call Henry. I had to inform Henry that I'd received the notice; it was company procedure. When I told him, I said nothing about which case I'd be sitting on. Henry immediately commented, "I'll bet it's for the O.J. Simpson case. It's got to be."

I just shrugged. Henry and I had what I always tried to dismiss as a "personality conflict." I never said any more or less to Henry than was necessary to conduct business. He signed the necessary paperwork allowing me to take the day off for jury selection; I thanked him and went on about my business.

Henry apparently kept quiet about my jury call. No one mentioned it to me. But one day everything changed dramatically. At Federal Express we have regular sessions called "loop meetings." At one of them, Henry floored me by suddenly announcing: "Did you guys know that Michael Knox is going to be sitting on the O.J. Simpson jury?''

I was stunned. Not really angry, because I hadn't asked Henry to keep it a secret. But he should have had the decency to ask me if I wanted it discussed. My co-workers started oohing and aahing and making catcalls for a few minutes. I hoped that would be the end of it, but as I walked away from the meeting, a fellow employee I'd known for years, a woman I'll call Marta, said loudly: ''Hey, hold on. I have a song I want to play for you.''

She walked towards me carrying a tape recorder, then said: ''I want you to sing this song to O.J. for me when you go down to the courthouse.''

What the hell is this, I thought. . . .

Marta punched the button on the tape recorder. It blasted out at full volume, and I heard the famed rhythm and blues singer, Sam Cooke, belting out his famous rendition of ''That's the Sound of the Man Working on the Chain Gang.''

I felt like I'd been hit by a physical blow. This would have been an unforgivable insult if a black person had committed it! Coming from a white woman, it was a vicious expression of racial contempt. The imagery of chain gangs to people who have suffered a legacy of slavery is a powerful symbol. Even a person hopelessly ignorant—which Marta is not—had to know an action like this would cause great pain.

I turned and walked away immediately. I couldn't leave for home because I still had work to complete. So I walked to another part of the work area, trying to avoid Marta. But she followed me, playing that damnable song relentlessly. She kept laughing and making nasty cracks: "O.J.'s gonna be breakin' rocks on that chain gang . . . he's gonna be doing hard time . . . you make sure you put him on that chain gang, Michael. . . ."

Stupidly, I kept trying to avoid her. When this nightmare had begun, several of my coworkers were witnesses to what was happening. But most of them just laughed uncertainly, the way people do when they don't want to face trouble or even acknowledge that something bad is happening.

Henry was right there, watching it all.

The expression on his face told me everything I needed to know. He was behind this. I'd get no help from him. He looked like a cat watching a mouse die.

Again, I can't tell you why I didn't just walk out of there. Some kind of macho pride, I guess. I moved to a more secluded part of the building, but Marta kept following. I knew she wanted to get a rise out of me, to watch me get angry and blow my stack. Instead, I said to her, "Don't you think this is very immature?" Looking back on it now, I wish I had ripped the tape recorder out of her hand and smashed it into a thousand pieces. But I didn't.

Marta harassed me with that Sam Cooke tape for nearly thirty minutes. That's another reason I know she had Henry's tacit backing. There's no way Henry would allow anyone who was supposed to be working to goof off for half an hour.

That night I went home and tried to figure it all out over a couple of beers. I didn't tell Beverly anything. I knew she'd be infuriated. Up until that day I'd never had any trouble at Federal Express. I'd worked there since

1987, starting out as a handler who loads trucks with packages and overnight letters that go to Los Angeles Airport every evening. After three years in that job I had applied for a promotion to courier. A courier is the person who comes to your home or office for deliveries and pickups. I was sent to courier school, then took a test and passed.

I'd worked for nearly five years at that job, so it's obvious the company approved of my work. I liked the job and it paid me $16.03 an hour. I got along great with everybody—even Marta. Or so I'd thought. Then Henry became my supervisor, and I knew from the get-go that I had trouble. The word had spread among the black couriers at Federal Express: The new white boss had racist attitudes.

I was never really sure if that was true about Henry. Racism can be a tough thing to detect. Sometimes it's far, far below the surface. I remember something that Roy Innes, the black leader and head of CORE (Congress of Racial Equality), had said in an interview. He talked about how white people usually wouldn't go into rages and riot when they were angry at black people. Instead, they would suppress it, hold it inside. Innes called it "the silent hate."

That silent hate is what I had seen on Henry's face when Marta followed me around my workplace playing that "Chain Gang" song.

It wasn't just that Henry hadn't tried to stop Marta's harassment of me. An unanswered question made me even more suspicious: How did Marta just happen to have a tape of that "Chain Gang" song handy if Henry hadn't told her beforehand that he was going to announce my O.J. jury call?

Sitting home alone that night, wrestling with all of this really unsettled me. It's amazing how important our jobs become to us, not just in terms of earning a living but as a defining center of our lives. Suddenly, the rhythm of my life had skipped a beat, changed its familiar pattern. Would it settle back into the same old familiar, comfortable groove tomorrow?

Over the next few days and weeks, everything started coming apart at Federal Express. As I said, I'd been a courier for about five years. I knew the job cold. But suddenly, I couldn't do anything right. Henry was on my case, and I knew he'd get me. Part of my job was preparing paperwork for international billing. It's not particularly difficult, but it can get tricky. There are codes we use to make sure the package or letter goes to the right city, state, or foreign country so that it's delivered and billed properly.

A white woman I'll call Lois had been put in charge of monitoring my paperwork and reporting on my efficiency to Henry. I had never had a complaint before, but now she was telling Henry that I wasn't getting the coding to international countries correct. For instance, she'd say, "Michael had two coding options for Australia. He assigned a code that got the package to Australia, but not to the right *station* in Australia."

After about a month of this, Henry called me into his office. He announced that what Federal Express calls a "performance letter" was being placed in my employee file. It cataloged the complaints against me and said that my work was not up to the standards required.

Henry told me, "Michael, you're getting this performance letter because you've miscoded a package. Let me warn you that we have a new rule now. If you have too many miscodes in a certain period of time, you are given the option of stepping down to a lower position. If you choose not to step down, you'll be fired after your next coding error."

I protested. "Henry, I just don't see why all of a sudden my work isn't satisfactory. I've never had any problems until Lois started looking over my work." Henry shrugged. "You'll just have to concentrate harder. You don't have any leeway to make more mistakes."

That night, I poured myself a stiff drink at home and tried to figure out how to handle this. Looking back on it now, I probably should have challenged Henry and made him show me exactly where I'd made mistakes. That's what my wife wanted me to do.

Beverly said, "Don't just take this lying down. How can you be working all these years and doing fine, then start making mistakes all of a sudden? It's crazy. Is there something you're not telling me?"

I hadn't told Beverly about the "Chain Gang" incident. I didn't want to worry her. But now it all came pouring out and I told her everything. She was furious.

"You know this is racist stuff, Michael. You've got to challenge them, make them see you're not going to back down without a fight."

"But baby, nothing I do can make any difference. They're down on me. It's the race thing, and that's that."

Beverly started crying angry tears. "Why have they started on you now like this . . . why?"

I shook my head. I felt like crying myself. "I don't know. It just all started with the O.J. thing."

"O.J. thing? Why are they blaming you for O.J.?"

"I guess it's because he killed two white people, and they want to make him pay. I guess they think that if I get on the jury, and I'm scared enough of losing my job, I'll vote against O.J."

"That's the craziest thing I ever heard. You aren't even on the jury yet."

I sighed. "Baby, I know it's crazy, and the more you try to make sense out of it, the crazier it sounds."

I put away a few drinks that night trying to figure a way out of this mess. Should I try going over Henry's head? No, that wouldn't work. What could I really prove? And if I went to the higher ups and couldn't make them believe me, my life on the job would be a living hell. No, I decided, I'd fight Henry another way.

The next morning I went back to work ready to put my new plan into action. It was simple: I was going to buckle down and concentrate so hard that I couldn't *possibly* make any mistakes.

It sounds naive now. And maybe what I was doing was a subconscious effort to avoid confrontation. But I really believed that if I focused totally on my work I wouldn't make a mistake. I knew my job really well, and I'd worked for years with no serious complaints. Surely if I made an extra effort even Lois wouldn't be able to find fault.

My plan failed. At Federal Express, it's almost impossible not to make a mistake from time to time. You're constantly interpreting customers' handwriting, so it's easy to misread a zip code and enter it into the computer wrong. Everybody there makes mistakes. And I'm not saying that I never made a mistake in five years as a courier. But I wasn't making any more mistakes than anybody else. If anything, I truly believe I was making fewer. But anyone who's ever worked knows that if a boss suddenly starts to really bear down on you—what they call micromanaging—he'll get you eventually.

About two weeks after my first performance letter, Henry called me into his office.

"Michael," he said, "I've got some bad news for you. You're getting another performance letter in your file. You've now got two options. You can either take a demotion to handler or you can continue in your job as a courier, but with the stipulation that if you make one more mistake, you'll be fired."

Henry gave me a thin little smile. I thought, You racist son of a bitch. Why do you hate me so much that you're willing to take food out of the mouths of my family? What the hell have I ever done to you?

I said, "Henry, this is wrong. You know it's wrong. Lois is riding me and you've obviously told her to do it. Why the hell is my work suddenly no good after all these years?"

"Michael, that's a question for you to answer, not me. Anyway, I've told you what your options are. Will you step down or not?"

There it was. Goddam. It's not that I was surprised. I'd known deep down that this was coming. But now that I actually faced what I'd been dreading, I felt pain and helpless anger in every part of me. Step down or gamble that Lois could never find another mistake that would get me fired? For me, it was a simple choice. Live today to fight tomorrow. My babies had to eat.

"I'll take the demotion, Henry."

Again, he smiled. "You understand that there's a substantial cut in pay?"

I thought, Yeah, you son of a bitch. Four bucks an hour. A 25 percent pay cut. Thank you, you lousy bastard.

I said: "Yes, I understand."

I walked out of Henry's office. I felt like going home, but I knew he'd probably use that as an excuse to fire me outright. As the day wore on, I got knowing looks from Lois and Marta. Over the past several weeks, Marta had played the "Chain Gang" tape several times. And made the usual cracks about O.J.

How I despised this woman. In all my years at Federal Express, I'd never had trouble with anyone. Strangely enough, I'd even considered Marta a friend—not a close friend, but a good work friend. It was so hard for me to fathom that the O.J. Simpson case had polarized some of these people so completely that they were willing to vent their rage on someone who'd never harmed them, who worked side by side with them day after day.

I dreaded telling Beverly what had happened. When I got home that night, I waited until the kids were all kissed good night and in bed. Then I sat her down and told her what we were facing. Beverly was great.

"It's not your fault, Michael, so don't go beating yourself up over it. I knew this would happen if you got involved in this O.J. thing. It's the biggest thing there is, and people just get really wrapped up in it. We'll get by. And now that those awful people have brought you down, I think they'll leave you alone."

Beverly was dead-on right. I started working as a handler and was no longer under Henry's supervision. Marta stopped playing the "Chain Gang" tape, and Lois never even looked in my direction again. The harassment was over.

One week later, I walked into my house whistling a happy tune. I couldn't help it. I felt damn good for a change. Beverly looked at me and said, "You just win the lottery or something?"

"No ma'am . . . I've just been picked for the O.J. Simpson jury."

8

⚖

Somewhere
Near Dodger
Stadium

JANUARY 11, 1995

8:10 A.M.

"Man, this is just like going to sixth grade camp."

"Oh, you're just looking forward to a vacation from me and the kids," said my wife Beverly, only half-joking.

Deep down, I felt a guilty twinge. After all the crap I'd gone through on my job, I admittedly felt relieved that I wouldn't have to look into the eyes of the tormentors who had demoted me. I shrugged and said: "Come on, baby. I'm just trying to make the best of a bad deal here. You know I'm going to miss you. What do you want me to do, act all gloomy?"

Actually, I felt cheerful, pumped up. That was amazing, because it was one hell of a gray, rainy day. It had poured all through the night. Beverly and I had been up late, packing my things. A few days before, we'd gotten a call from the court clerks to gather at a secret spot near Dodger Stadium.

It was on a side street and all the jurors were there, bags packed. Family members milled around, everybody kissing each other good-bye. Passing motorists got curious looks on their faces as they spotted the armed and uniformed sheriff's deputies surrounding us. Finally, the deputies took a head count. We were all present—twelve jurors and twelve alternates. The deputies gave us a five-minute countdown to get our farewells completed, then stepped forward and gently herded us toward three white vans with tinted windows that were parked at the curb. We all piled in, twenty-four strangers who were about to become a team for justice; not knowing exactly where we were heading, just that it was a hotel God-knows-where.

It was a tight squeeze in the vans. The deputies told us: "There is too much luggage to get it all in one trip. We'll leave someone here to guard your stuff. It will take one or two extra trips to get it all to your destination, so there will be a delay on the other end. But we'll make sure you get your luggage."

As the vans pulled away from the curb, we peered from the windows and waved back at our families. Finally, we couldn't see them anymore—and suddenly, we were officially a part of O.J. history. Sequestered. Isolated. Alone among strangers.

For a long moment, there was silence. Then, like a switch had been thrown, everybody started talking at once.

"I wonder where they'll put us up?"

"I hope the food is good. Do you think they'll have diet meals? Because I only eat . . ."

". . . no newspapers. That's gonna be hard to take . . ."

". . . couldn't believe it when I got those

written instructions a couple of weeks ago saying you couldn't have tape recorders, radios, or CDs."

"I have to laugh every time I think about my husband cooking his own meals."

"This hotel better not be a dump . . ."

That van ride was one of the friendliest times the O.J. jurors ever had. It was as if we'd been launched in little spaceships, heading out into the unknown on some mysterious mission. I felt good, but slightly apprehensive. We all did. That's why we couldn't stop babbling. Finally, we arrived at the hotel. What a pleasant surprise. It was a first-class establishment. Everybody gave a little cheer and somebody said, "Thanks, Judge Ito!"

Everybody nodded in agreement. Maybe this sequestration wouldn't be so bad. The deputies unloaded us in the underground parking garage and we were whisked up to one of the two floors reserved exclusively for the jury. That's when any illusion that we were in an adult version of summer camp vanished. This was army boot camp—or day one in prison.

The first shock was being searched. Suddenly the deputies were ordering us to "Line up over here, please. It is necessary that we search you and your luggage. We are going to ask you to go through a metal detector . . . ."

Man, what a thorough search! They went through our luggage slowly, deliberately, examining everything.

I'll never forget one electric moment when the deputies found bullets in the luggage of a great big guy named Fred. Turned out it was no big deal. He'd absentmindedly left them in his suitcase after a hunting trip.

I managed to smuggle in one piece of contraband—my little pocketknife. I'm a great believer in the tradition that red-blooded American boys should carry a pocketknife at all times. I didn't feel a shred of guilt for beating the system that day. How did I do it? Like any good magician, I'm not going to reveal my tricks but the hand IS quicker than the eye! To be honest, the reason I didn't surrender my pocketknife was because I suddenly resented being "locked down" like a common criminal. That's exactly what was happening, and that's how I still describe it. It was no way to treat citizens, and none of us liked it. Hiding that pocketknife was my personal rebellion.

"Can you believe this?" I muttered to a juror named Carl. "I feel like the next thing they're going to do is hose us down, delouse us, and shave our heads."

While we were lined up in the hotel corridor, I made small talk with Carl and Fred. Other jurors also began talking to each other while we waited out the luggage search, and I noticed a curious thing: We were starting to act like prison cons, talking low and not moving our lips very much. I don't want to exaggerate; it wasn't like a Jimmy Cagney prison movie, but there was a subtle change in our behavior when we realized that deputies were always positioning themselves so that they could eavesdrop on our conversations. Perhaps "eavesdrop" is the wrong word. But they had been ordered to monitor all our conversations.

I kept up my chitchat with Carl and Fred—until I discovered that Carl had REALLY bad breath. I turned to Fred and learned that he, like myself, was an ex-track and field athlete. He still coached high school teams around Los Angeles County. We chatted as the luggage search went on, then the deputies issued us room keys, lined us up, and marched us to our rooms, one by one.

Inside the rooms, the search process continued. We were "patted down" by deputies of our own sex. It was demeaning and exhausting. And every couple of minutes during that first day, we keep hearing deputies drone on and on about the "rules." We'd get speeches like: "No juror will be allowed to enter the room of any other juror at any time. There are no exceptions to this rule. If you wish to have contact with another juror you may call them on the house phone. Or if that is inconvenient, you can approach the juror's room, knock, then step back and stand at a minimum distance of three feet from the door. When the juror comes to the door you may have a brief conversation. If you wish to have social contact you can invite the juror to join you in one of the common areas, such as the video room or the lounge."

Breaking the rules was a near impossibility. That first day we had about ten deputies helping us get settled in. In the days and weeks to come, there were always at least seven patrolling the floors. Deputies were always posted in the telephone room, in the lounge, and in the corridors at each entrance and elevator bank. That first night I called home and told Beverly: "It's really weird. They've got eyes on you every minute. The only privacy you get is in your room. But they don't let you hook the chain inside the door, so they could walk in on you anytime."

"You mean they have keys to your rooms?"

"Of course they have keys, Beverly. If they think you somehow got hold of anything you're not suppose to have, like newspapers with stuff about the trial, they're just going to go into your room and search— whether you're there or not. They watch everything you do and hear everything you say. There's a deputy standing here right now, listening to this conversation."

I waved my hand at the female deputy

who happened to be monitoring the phone conversations that night. She gave me one of those "Ha, Ha . . . NOT FUNNY!" looks.

"Well, least I know those deputies won't let any female jurors in your room," Beverly said sarcastically.

"That's right, baby," I laughed. "All you have to worry about is one of the female deputies taking a liking to me. I have to obey orders, you know—and these girls have guns."

"Mmm, hhmm! Well, you keep your gun in your holster, mister."

That first day was a shocker—especially when all the jurors sat down for lunch, our very first meal together, at about 2:30 in the afternoon. It was a late lunch because we'd had to complete the endless indoctrination process. After it was over, the deputies lined us up and marched us down to the fourth floor dining room that would be ours exclusively.

When we sat down, an amazing thing happened: There was an immediate separation of the races. It was so impromptu, happening so naturally, that I'm convinced to this day it was not preconceived on anyone's part. One minute we were a melting pot; the next, three separate tables, islands segregated according to race. Black jurors at one table. Black alternate jurors at another table. Whites and Latinos at yet another table.

It was eerie! All during lunch, people made polite chitchat about how good the food was, how the hotel seemed very nice, etc. But not one comment was made about the unspoken decision to segregate according to race.

After lunch I spoke to one of the jurors, a woman named Millie. I said, "You know it's just like on the outside. We have our separation out there and it carries over in here."

Millie shrugged. "You're right. That's just the way it is, unfortunately."

I met Tracy Hampton that first day. Tracy is an attractive, twenty-five-year-old airline stewardess who seemed strangely shy and unsure of herself for someone whose job throws her into constant contact with people.

Unlike most of us black jurors, Tracy had the mannerisms and style of someone born with the proverbial silver spoon in her mouth. She talked differently. In street slang, we call it "sounding white." As I got to know Tracy, I learned she was the daughter of an upper-middle-class black family who lived in Ladera Heights, and that she'd attended schools that were predominately white. After that first lunch, Tracy quietly asked me if I had noticed the segregation at the tables.

"Yes, I did notice it," I said.

"They don't like black people," Tracy said, shaking her head.

"Well, Tracy, maybe it's just because folks tend to congregate with people like themselves. You know, all of us black people sat at one table because we have things in common we can share."

Tracy wasn't convinced by my Pollyanna explanation. "I experienced segregation as a flight attendant. It was just like what happened here today. Things never change."

"What happened to you?"

"Oh, lots of things. I remember when I was just starting out, I worked a flight to

Paris. I'd never been there before, so when the other flight attendants went out to get something to eat and do some shopping I tagged along with them. But they ditched me right in the middle of Paris. I mean, one minute I turned around and they just weren't there. I had to find my own way back to the hotel and I didn't speak any French. That's how whites are going to treat you every time."

9

⚖️
Jury Profiles

Tracy Hampton
    Juror Number 453, Dismissed
    An African-American female, age twenty-six, extremely attractive, has worked as an airline flight attendant.

    Tracy is a naive young woman. Although she doesn't realize it herself, she talks and acts like a white Valley Girl. She's well educated, from a very good family. But she's not as streetwise as some of the other black female jurors.

    Tracy is your basic "mama's girl." She's very concerned with how people perceive her and was always asking me how she looked every day. Very concerned about her personal image. We became very good friends.

Lisa

Juror Number 44

African-American female in her late thirties. A postal worker whose husband is in the navy. Lisa was the comedienne of the group and kept almost everybody laughing. But there were some on that jury that even Lisa couldn't get a smile out of. She was not only very funny, but very smart. And she could become extremely serious.

Millie

Juror Number 37

African-American female, age about fifty. Works for Los Angeles County in an administrative job. Millie is very well spoken, very well educated and carries herself in a very dignified way. She is the kind of person people look up to and respect. Millie's always been my choice for jury foreman and I'll bet that she's the one the other jurors choose. Despite her great dignity, Millie has a terrific personality. There's nothing stuffy or high-hat about her. In fact, she and Lisa were the best of friends, even though Lisa's a real comedienne. Younger jurors viewed her as sort of a surrogate mom. Millie and I were very good friends.

Jeanette Harris

Juror Number 94, Dismissed

African-American female, age thirty-eight. Works as an employment counselor. Jeanette's a tough lady. She's well groomed, presents a pleasant appearance, but she's very reserved and watchful. Jeanette comes across as street smart, rather than book smart. She's usually very quiet. But after you've been around Jeanette for awhile, you realize she's taking everything in and making a judgment. Jeanette sends her messages by her eloquent eyes and her body language. I have seen Jeanette freeze somebody dead just by the tiniest shift in the way she's sitting or standing, and by the unmistakable message in those piercing eyes of hers. A vindictive lady. You learn not to get on her bad side.

Mr. Johnson

Juror Number 76

African-American male, age about seventy. Mr. Johnson is a kindly man who strikes you as someone you'd like to get to know better. Sadly, Mr. Johnson cannot abide white people. He was raised in the Deep South and experienced quite a bit of racism when he was growing up. These experiences formed him as a man. As long as the subject of white people doesn't arise, Mr. Johnson is a perfect gentleman. On questions of race, as I discovered, he's a keg of dynamite.

Tracy Kennedy, aka "T.K."

Juror Number 88, Dismissed

White male, age about fifty-six. A highly intelligent man with a background in engineering. Yet T.K. was totally obnoxious. Not one juror I can think of liked him, especially the black jurors. And especially Mr. Johnson. He could get agitated just by looking at T.K. That's because the man was a dead ringer for Colonel Sanders, with his white hair, white moustache, and pointed face. Even worse, T.K. had what black people call a "massa" attitude that would drive them right up the wall. T.K. never stopped pushing. He came barreling onto the jury wanting to be fore-man even before we were seated. He ended up being thrown off the jury. That says it all about T.K.

Farron Chavarria

Juror Number 81, Dismissed

A Latina female in her late twenties, Farron works in real estate. She's quiet, well spoken, and extremely businesslike. She was known for taking voluminous notes. In conversations with her, I got the strong impression that she was pro-prosecution. She told me she's a former aerobics instructor. One of her best pals on the jury was Francine Florio-Bunten.

Willie Cravin

Juror Number 64, Dismissed

A big, hulking guy in his fifties, Willie is a former high school athlete who holds a management position in the post office. Willie loves to talk about his past glories as an athlete. He exposed himself as a bully almost from the start, menacing jurors who spoke when he wanted silence, and he threatened me physically.

10 ⚖️

Boxed In

The racial segregation at mealtimes continued. It was sort of like everybody was choosing up sides. Six black jurors sat at one table, six white jurors sat at the adjacent table. A mixed bag of black and white alternate jurors sat at yet another table toward the rear of the dining room. It started to bother me. I thought, What's it going to be like if we all keep separating according to race?

Lisa kept talking about insisting on conjugal visits. "I don't know about the rest of you, but I'm going to get mighty tense and awful hard to live with if Judge Ito doesn't let us have those conjugal visits," she laughed.

Somebody said, "Lisa, you just got here.

Don't you think it's a little early to start worrying about that?"

"Honey, it's never too early to start planning."

The hotel we were sequestered at was first class. But little things reminded us that this was not a vacation and we were not normal guests. For instance, there were no phones in our rooms. There were no security chains on the insides of the doors—a fact that would eventually cause paranoia and suspicion. And the TV sets were not connected. If you wanted to watch a videotape, you had to go to the video room.

But the restriction that annoyed me most of all was that we weren't allowed to have drink in the evening. I can understand Judge Ito not wanting a bunch of rip-roaring drunk jurors. But why couldn't we have a couple of beers or wine? The deputies could easily have monitored intake. It was infuriating to be treated like children.

You couldn't leave the hotel, of course.

We were allowed out into a secure patio area once in awhile. But the corridors were so long on our private floors that you could jog and get exercise that way. We even had a curfew—11:00 P.M. on weeknights and 12:00 midnight on the weekends. If you were in your room, you could stay up all night if you chose. It was going to be a long, lonely haul.

At 5:30 A.M. sharp, you'd hear a knock on your door. A deputy would yell out, "One hour to breakfast." That got to be a real drag. A white female alternate juror named Francine complained loud and long about getting up that early for breakfast, then rushing over to the courthouse to hang out until we were called. "Why can't we have breakfast at the courthouse?" she used to ask.

It was a reasonable suggestion. Once we became familiar with the courthouse downtown, we realized that meals were served on the eleventh floor where we used to congregate before going to the ninth floor jury room. There was nothing wrong with the food at the hotel. It was excellent. It was the morning routine that bothered us. Again, it was like military boot camp. After the deputies woke you up, you'd fall out of bed and get ready to face the day. Then we'd all assemble out in the hallway in single file. Everybody had to wait until every last juror was out in the hallway and lined up ready to go. Then the deputies would march us down to the fourth floor dining room. Lining up to wait for a bus was one thing—but lining up to be marched off to a meal somehow felt demeaning.

Finally, Francine wrote a letter to Judge Ito. And he gave us permission to have our breakfast at the courthouse. Most of us were thrilled that Francine had written the letter. It changed our morning routine for the better. But right away, Jeanette Harris started muttering that Francine should have consulted with everyone first—even though we'd all talked about it informally and agreed it was a great idea. It was ridiculous, but that's how Jeanette seemed to react to any situation that she hadn't initiated. Frankly, I think she liked the new breakfast arrangements as much as any of us. But Jeanette had to be queen bee—or somebody got stung!

That first couple of weeks before we became involved in courtroom proceedings turned miserable for all of us. My household is populated by kids who can be a handful and a dog, so I'd secretly been looking forward to this as a sort of a vacation. I hadn't visualized how boring it would be. No TV, no radio, no shopping trips, no jaunts to the beach or the ball game. For the first three or four weeks, we weren't even allowed to go outside. Just think of it—*no* recreation! When we were finally allowed to visit the patio area of the hotel and take a swim in the pool, I almost went nuts with the pleasure of it all.

But the worst part of being sequestered was not seeing new faces. Despite the problems I'd had at my workplace, there were still friendly faces there I missed. Human beings are social animals and isolation of any kind, even for a day or two, can depress us. Enforced, ongoing intimacy with two dozen strangers wears you down. When we started going to the courtroom, things got a little better. But after a week or two, you realized you were still seeing the same old surroundings and faces, day after day. And even though the drama of the trial proceedings could get very exciting, ask yourself this: When you had your TV set tuned into the O.J. trial via CNN, Court TV, or the E! Entertainment channel, did you watch intently, every minute? Or did you get up and leave the room when the lawyers got tedious or technical?

Perhaps we O.J. jurors were a bunch of malcontents, crybabies who somehow ended up in the same group. But I don't think so. That's why it's no surprise to me that we were the first jury in American history to revolt against the court.

_____

After awhile, cliques began to form. Lisa, Millie, and I were always joking and laughing. Jeanette and a black female juror named Pamela grew very close. Tracy Hampton, who was usually too shy to say much around the others, would often sit with me and chat in the lounge. Mr. Johnson and Carl would talk endlessly about the boorish and obnoxious antics of T.K.

In the first week or two, as we sized each other up, I realized that the constant back-and-forth banter between Lisa, Millie, and myself was beginning to annoy Jeanette and Pamela. Conversation was an art they neither practiced nor appreciated. The three of us sensed that the two of them were smoldering. But the four-alarm fire didn't start until Mr. Johnson joined our table.

Mr. Johnson was an alternate juror who chose to sit at the alternates' table—not that there was any rule that he, or anyone, for that matter, had to sit in any particular place. One of the jurors at our table, I think it was Jeanette, had asked Mr. Johnson to sit with us. But he'd made it plain that he wouldn't because he believed that one of the black male jurors had a "lifestyle" he found distasteful. When that juror was released early on because he'd worked for Hertz—the same company that had employed O.J. Simpson as a media spokesman—Mr. Johnson joined the black jurors' table.

Trouble started immediately. Mr. Johnson, a man set in his ways, believed that the best way to savor good food was in complete silence. It wasn't long before he and Lisa clashed. One night he said to her: "Lisa, do you have to be so loud?"

Lisa put down her fork and stared coolly at the old man. "What do you mean 'so loud'?"

"You know what I mean," said Mr. Johnson. "What's wrong with you? Why do you always have to act so silly?"

The whole table fell silent. I looked around. Jeanette had a smug, self-satisfied look on her face. Lisa leaned forward and looked Mr. Johnson right in the eye.

"This is the way I am, Mr. Johnson," she said with quiet force. "If you can't accept that, sir, I suggest you just go back to the table you came from and sit there."

Wow! It was a tense moment. Nobody moved. Mr. Johnson glared, but Lisa never dropped her gaze. Finally, Mr. Johnson lowered his eyes to his plate. He picked up his fork, then said: "I just wish you guys would pipe down a little bit. You know, it's time to eat here. I don't think we need all this noise and carrying on."

Nobody said a word. There was nothing

to be said. It was one of the most uncomfortable moments I've ever experienced. I glanced at Jeanette just as she and Lisa exchanged a look that said it all. The battle lines were drawn. Mealtimes weren't going to be pleasant times anymore.

I'll never know what makes people like Jeanette Harris tick; pompous, self-centered folks who believe they should control all the lives around them. They exist to manipulate, dominate. I remembered reading that in the 1988 domestic abuse complaint she'd filed against her husband—the incident she'd failed to reveal on her jury questionnaire—Jeanette claimed that her husband threatened her because she'd refused to have sex with him. I don't know the truth of her complaint, but it's a scene I could imagine—Jeanette, smug and vengeful, observing her husband's rage as she informed him that she would withhold the intimacy of the marriage.

In a conversation about the clash between Lisa and Mr. Johnson at the dinner table, someone commented on how Jeanette had raked the table with her eyes.

"That woman's got a stare that feels like an ass-whipping!"

Jeanette's favorite "whipping boy" was a woman: Tracy Hampton. After a few meals together, it became apparent that Jeanette and her pal, Pamela, were deliberately ignoring Tracy. They'd talk around her, never speaking to her directly. And even when she tried to join the conversation by asking a direct question, she'd be ignored. Maybe Tracy was learning that those white flight attendants in Paris weren't the only ones that could be cold and unfriendly. Unfriendly black folks can be as unfriendly as unfriendly white folks. Their behavior began to wear Tracy down. I tried to comfort her, saying she should just ignore the freeze out. But Tracy, who wanted so desperately to be liked, just couldn't understand that was out of her control.

"What have I done to her, Michael?" she'd ask, distraught and near tears. "I try to be nice, but she just won't talk to me. None of them will. Why are they treating me this way?"

"Tracy, stop acting like you've done

something wrong. It's got nothing to do with you. Jeanette knows she can control you. She knows how much it upsets you to be ignored. That's why she's doing what she's doing. And you're just making it easy for her by acting as if it affects you. Everybody can see you're upset, and that's just what Jeanette wants."

"Oh, Michael, this is so horrible! I hate it here. I just want to go home. I don't know why I ever agreed to be on this jury. Do you think I can ask the judge to go home?"

"Tracy, the best way to deal with this is to act like you don't have a care in the world. If you just act natural, like Jeanette isn't ignoring you, she'll get tired of it and she won't have any control over you."

Tears sprang into Tracy's eyes. "I hate it here, Michael. I've just got to get out of here."

Witnessing Tracy's torment made me feel angry and helpless. It was subtle and relentless. And no one could do a damn thing about it. In a conversation with Lisa, she told me that Jeanette's antagonism towards Tracy was a natural female kind of jealousy. Jeanette is not an unattractive woman. But she was no match for Tracy, who had looks and sex appeal in abundance. Millie, when I appealed to her for help, said part of the problem was jealousy. That surprised me, but Lisa said: "You think Jeanette's just doing it because she likes to be in control. That's true, but you're a man and you just don't see the threat that someone who looks like Tracy can be to a woman. Women always compete for the attention of males, and Jeanette resents the attention that you and the other guys give to Tracy."

Another strange thing happened after we'd been sequestered for awhile. Even though mealtimes had become somewhat unpleasant because of all the undercurrents, the food at the hotel was excellent. And there was plenty of it—too much, in fact. Three big meals got to be just too much. Some jurors asked if they could opt to stay in their rooms rather than eat every meal. But the deputies wouldn't allow it. You had to show up for every meal for a head count, they told us. You could sit and play with your food, or even not eat it, but you had to be at the table for every meal.

Looking at notes I kept in the early days of sequestration, the entry for Thursday, January 12, reads: "Now I know what O.J. must feel like. Nothing to do, nowhere to go. Only the second day, yet a lot of us are starting to have problems. Hotel very nice, but it's like prison. Always told where to go. All meals eaten in same room. Four or five deputies escort us from our rooms on the fifth floor down to our meal room, located on the fourth floor. Marching in single file up and down the stairs. Deputy at every doorway. No contact with anybody else in the hotel. Only with one another."

Even in those first few days, I sat and wondered why none of us had anticipated the sheer misery of being in a sequestered jury. The answer? Because no one in the court system had leveled with us. It's not that they were trying to hide the truth. After all, we knew that we'd be locked away in a hotel, isolated from family and friends, possibly without conjugal visits.

But nobody emphasized that we'd actually be worse off than prison inmates, with deputies monitoring not just our activities, but our conversations. Somehow, the phrase "monitoring conversations" doesn't adequately describe the reality—that Big Brother will be eavesdropping on virtually ever word you utter. Even prisoners are allowed to speak privately.

Stop and think about that! Think back on every conversation you've had in the last twenty-four hours. Now imagine that every word you've said—every confidence shared with friends, every nasty crack uttered about your boss, every catty remark made behind the back of an enemy or friend—is being tape recorded and reported to the authorities. The unpleasant reality was that deputies listened in on nearly every word we said as we marched to and from meals, watched videos, played cards, or had intimate phone conversations. It was devastating!

The deputies? In time, we would learn more about the human beings behind those authority symbols, the badges and guns. For the moment, they were just uniforms, and you twitched when you spotted them out of the corner of your eye.

Paranoia sprang up everywhere. Millions of Americans heard news reports about excused juror Jeanette Harris's complaint to Judge Ito that she thought our rooms were being searched. It was a legitimate concern. One night, while I was sitting with Tracy Hampton in the lounge, she looked around furtively to make sure that no deputies were standing within earshot. Then she said: "Michael, I think my room is being searched."

I looked at her in utter amazement. "Tracy, don't you think you're maybe a bit paranoid?" I said. "They've already searched our stuff. We haven't been outside yet, so why would they search us so soon again?"

"I don't know, Michael. Maybe they think we hide things from them or . . . maybe . . ."

"Or what?"

"Well . . ." She hesitated, looking agitated. "You know, maybe I'm the only one they're looking at . . . you know?"

"What are you talking about, girl? What are you trying to say?"

"Well, it's just that I'm the youngest female and . . . well, I think some of these male deputies are getting ideas. I think they've been coming into my room."

"You mean, they're spying on you? Like, cracking open your door and peeking at you?" I asked, incredulous.

Tracy got upset. "You sound like you don't believe me. Why do you think that's so impossible, with them watching every move we make? I've seen how they look at me. And how do I know what happens when I'm asleep at night? There are no chain locks on our doors."

Man, this was some deep stuff. One part of me thought Tracy was paranoid. But after experiencing the way the court and the deputies had taken over some of even the most private parts of our lives, I didn't want to be too quick to dismiss her suspicions as girlish silliness.

"Tracy, if you have no evidence of this, how can you? . . ."

"I never said I didn't have proof, Michael."

She looked around again, then lowered

her voice to a whisper. "When I first felt like my things were being searched, I put something in my room in a certain position, so I'd know if anyone had been messing with it. When I went back to look, it had been moved. It's driving me crazy, Michael. How can I sleep if I think someone may be coming in the room to spy on me? I hate this. I want to go home."

No matter how hard I tried, I couldn't calm Tracy down. Was she just being paranoid? I'll never know for sure. But I started watching the male deputies whenever she was around. I'm not saying that they never eyed her, but the glances she got were few and far between. I saw no evidence that any of the deputies had a fixation. But Tracy never stopped believing that someone was entering her room. And what made it worse was that the room she'd been assigned was adjacent to a guard post where deputies congregated.

The pressure finally eased up somewhat when two jurors—a Hispanic woman and the African-American male Hertz employee— were released from jury duty. Tracy promptly asked for, and got, a new room assignment.

"Oh Michael, I slept so much better last

night," she told me after her first night in the new room. "I always worried when they were standing in front of my room twenty-four hours a day. Oh, I feel so much better."

It's painful today to look back on that moment. Anyone who doubts the grinding psychological pressure of our jury ordeal only needs to look at the tragedies Tracy Hampton suffered after her release from the jury—reports of self-mutilation, attempted suicide, and prolonged hospitalization. I'll bet I'm not the only juror who felt a twinge of guilt about Tracy after hearing about her breakdown. Perhaps I should have listened to her fears with a more sympathetic ear, insisting that she inform Judge Ito, instead of believing she was a mama's girl with a hyperactive imagination. But my conscience is clear on one point; I never caused her pain, as others did.

Were there grounds for Tracy's fears that her room was being searched? At least one other juror, in addition to Jeanette Harris, believed that deputies were searching our rooms repeatedly. Nobody had any hard evidence. But T.K. was later dismissed from the jury for allegedly having a partially completed book about the O.J. jury in his possession. How was this unearthed, if not by systematic searches?

T.K. is one juror I keep thinking of when I recall those first days of jury selection and sequestration. Despite the fact that many of us found Tracy Kennedy obnoxious and rude, he was a compelling personality. In the first days after we were sequestered—in fact, I think it was the first day—Tracy came barreling up to me and said: "We've got to get together and decide who is going to be jury foreman. I'm the guy to do it right, because I have the managerial background and the computer expertise. I want you to support me."

I raised my eyebrows. Talk about coming on strong! I said, "I don't understand. What does computer expertise have to do with it?"

"Judge Ito allowed me to bring my computer with me, I've got it right here," he said. "I can keep us organized."

Then T.K. launched into a bizarre monologue. I can't remember the exact words, but his implication was clear: He wanted to write a book and make some big money.

"We've all got to look out for ourselves and look to the future, Mike," he said winking broadly. "You and I should talk about that some time."

I almost laughed out loud. Not at his idea, but at the cocky, confident way he expected a total stranger to buy into his dreams. Later, I said to Millie, "I just can't believe that T.K.! He's already talking about getting himself elected as jury foreman."

Millie laughed. "That's nothing," she said. "He approached me and said we should start discussing who was going to be the jury foreman—and that was even before he was selected to be on the jury."

11 ⚖️

Trial Chronology

JANUARY 11–JANUARY 18, 1995

Wednesday
January 11, 1995

1st day of sequestration

• Today the twelve jurors and twelve alternates began their sequestration at an undisclosed location.

Jury not present

• In court, the domestic violence issues were argued by both sides before Judge Lance Ito, with no jury present. The prosecution detailed a long history of incidents involving abuse of Nicole Brown Simpson by O.J. Simpson.

The defense, with argument by Gerald Uelmen, sought to exclude evidence of "domestic discord."

Thursday
January 12, 1995

2nd day of sequestration
Jury not present

• The prosecution withdrew eighteen of the original sixty-one alleged abuse incidents allegedly perpetrated by O.J. upon Nicole.

• Prosecutors advanced the theory that victim Ronald Goldman was killed because O.J. believed Goldman was romantically involved with Nicole.

• Prosecution called witness Donald Dutton, an expert on domestic violence.

• Famed criminal attorney F. Lee Bailey made his first appearance for the defense team, as he cross-examined Dutton.

Friday
January 13, 1995

3rd day of sequestration
Jury not present

• The race issue dominated at the O.J. Simpson trial as prosecutor Christopher Darden and defense lawyer Johnnie Cochran engaged in an emotional exchange.

• Two jurors were dismissed by Judge Ito; a thiryt-eight-year-old Latina postal worker and a forty-eight-year-old African-American employed by Hertz.

Saturday
January 14, 1995

4th day of sequestration

Sunday
January 15, 1995

5th day of sequestration

Monday
January 16, 1995

6th day of sequestration
Court not in session

• A reported rift in the O.J. Simpson defense team apparently came to a head only days before opening statements are scheduled to begin. The controversy involved a falling-out between Robert Shapiro and F. Lee Bailey, two longtime friends.

Tuesday
January 17, 1995

7th day of sequestration
Court not in session

• Opening statements expected to begin

today were rescheduled for Thursday, January 19.

• In a motion unsealed today, prosecutors stated that O.J. Simpson had hit his first wife, Marguerite Simpson Thomas, approximately twenty years ago, and police were called.

Wednesday
January 18, 1995

8th day of sequestration
Jury present

• Judge Lance Ito officially dismissed two jurors today and replaced them with randomly drawn alternates. All the jurors arrived at court together, but the two were excused separately out of hearing of the panel. Two alternates, a white female, sixty-three, who is a legal secretary, and an African-American male, forty-three, who works as a marketing representative, were seated.

- Jurors asked for and received permission for conjugal visits.

Jury not present

- In an important decision, Judge Ito ruled today that much of the domestic violence evidence will be admitted.

- Any relative of a victim will be excluded from the courtroom when another family member is testifying, if that relative is going to testify about the same matter.

- Judge Ito announced that opening statements scheduled to begin tomorrow morning will again be delayed. Monday, January 23, is the new start-up date.

Outside of court

- The defense team, thought to be in internal disarray, made a show of solidarity today by coming to court side by side, arm in arm, in lock step.

It has become noticeable that Robert Shapiro is deferring to Johnnie Cochran, who will now take the leading role in the trial for the defense.

12

⚖️

Judge Ito's Courtroom: First Day with O.J.

JANUARY 18, 1995

The big day had finally arrived. Suddenly, there we all were, filing into the jury box. Every face in the courtroom turned toward us. It was an electric moment. I'll never forget the weird feeling that swept over me as I suddenly found myself in a scene that had become so familiar, so vivid to millions of American TV viewers. It was as if I'd been watching a play and had suddenly found myself onstage, waiting for my first cue.

How familiar it all looked. Yet how different. On TV, the courtroom somehow seemed more imposing. Now it looked smaller, cramped. Everyone appeared to be tightly packed together; spectators, attorneys, the press, and the jury. Sitting above it all was Judge Ito, the one man who had lots of elbowroom.

I didn't focus on O.J. Simpson until I'd settled into my seat. I remember feeling almost shy about looking at him directly. Somehow I sensed that when I finally looked in his direction, he'd be looking right back at me—at us, the jury. I turned toward him and we made eye contact. He smiled slightly. I had to turn away. It felt . . . I don't know . . . strange. People talk of O.J.'s charisma. It hits like a hammer, believe me. I knew we all felt it as he surveyed us. He was confident, poised, with an ingratiating smile that just missed being childlike. The charm was undeniable, yet came up short of feeling completely natural. O.J.'s like a salesman selling a product he believes in totally—himself.

I thought, Here's a man on trial for a horrible crime and I've been chosen to sit in judgment of him. This isn't play-acting. It's as serious as life gets. I just hope I can do a good job. God, don't let me make any mistakes.

O.J.'s eyes were still sending messages. Whenever he'd look in your direction, you felt like he'd singled you out. I knew, of course, that he was looking at everyone on the jury. But somehow you felt that he was looking right at you. I broke my gaze and looked over at the reporters sitting in the front of the courtroom. Every eye in the press was leveled at the jury box. I almost laughed out loud when I realized they were watching us watch O.J. And they were actually taking notes about our reactions. Some artists were sketching us. Now I felt what O.J. Simpson probably feels every day of his high-powered life as a star who knows that every eye is on him. For me, the phenomenon would end with this trial. For O.J., no matter what happened in this trial, fame was forever.

Then I realized Judge Ito had started to speak. . . .

". . . like to welcome you, ladies and gentlemen of the jury . . ."

Judge Ito made general remarks, told us what to expect that day and gave us various guidelines. We learned that two of the jurors—an Hispanic woman and an African-American male—had been removed from the jury and were being replaced by two alternate jurors, a white female and an African-American male.

That's when Juror Number 353, an alternate juror, got a big laugh. Francine Florio-Bunten is a thirty-eight-year-old white woman who works as a technician for Pacific Bell, and she's always a crack-up! She made it very clear she approved of Judge Ito's decision to allow conjugal visits. I think she said something like, "I was thinking of tying my bed sheets together and slipping out of the hotel." It got a huge laugh. That put all of us jurors in a good mood. We looked around at each other, smiled, and nodded. I made a mental note to call Beverly that night to tell her the good news about our conjugal visits. Then I realized that she, like the rest of America, was out there watching on national TV. And she'd be reading all about us in the newspapers tomorrow. Ironically, we'd be the only ones who wouldn't be reading all about it.

I'd asked Beverly to save newspaper clips

that mentioned anything about the jury. I wanted to have clippings for a scrapbook. But I told her, "Don't try to save everything on the O.J. trial or you'll have the whole house filled up in no time. Just save stuff that mentions the jury. I don't imagine there'll be much mentioning us, so it shouldn't be a big job."

Who would have predicted that before very long, the jury itself would be making front-page headlines, day after day.

Another funny note: When we got back to the jury room, the deputies told us that our first conjugal visit would be Saturday, January 28, and we would be allowed five hours with our spouses or partners. Francine got the last laugh again. "That's four and a half hours more than my old man needs," she laughed.

Then, as everyone cracked up laughing, she got a little flustered and begged, "Don't any of you go telling my husband what I just said, O.K.?"

13 | ⚖️
Trial Chronology

JANUARY 19–JANUARY 24, 1995

Thursday
January 19, 1995

9th day of sequestration
Jury not present

• Trial was scheduled to begin today but due to unfinished business, opening statements are now rescheduled.

• Judge Ito is expected to decide tomorrow whether the defense can question Detective Mark Fuhrman regarding racist statements he allegedly made earlier in his career.

Friday
January 20, 1995

10th day of sequestration
Jury not present

• Judge Ito ruled today that lawyers for O.J. Simpson will not be permitted to question Det. Mark Fuhrman about racist remarks allegedly made during a workers' compensation case in 1981. Nor will they be allowed to ask questions pertaining to claims that Det. Fuhrman moved or planted evidence in a 1988 officer involved shooting case.

• Judge Ito said he may allow questions regarding racist remarks allegedly made by Mark Fuhrman as reported by real estate agent Kathleen Bell. The judge withheld a final ruling on that issue.

Saturday
January 21, 1995

11th day of sequestration

Sunday
January 22, 1995

12th day of sequestration

Monday
January 23, 1995

13th day of sequestration
Jury not present

• Scheduled to start this morning, opening statements were again postponed.

• Prosecutors accused defense counsel of withholding evidence in order to sabotage the state's case.

• The defense filed an unusual motion to allow the defendant, O.J. Simpson, to give a one-minute statement to the jury. Further, the defense requested that O.J. be allowed to approach the jury box to show his scars, injuries, and possible physical limitations.

• Judge Ito ruled that defense attorneys may cross-examine Det. Mark Fuhrman about his alleged racial slurs against African Americans. He also ruled that in the opening statements the defense will not be permitted to claim that Mark Fuhrman may have planted the bloody glove found at O.J.'s Brentwood estate.

• Opening statements are now scheduled to begin tomorrow.

Tuesday
January 24, 1995

14th day of sequestration
Jury present

• Today the long-awaited opening statement began. Christopher Darden was the first prosecutor to address the jury. He was followed by Marcia Clark.

• The defense opening statements were delayed when the Court TV camera accidentally showed an eight-tenths of a second flash of an alternate juror. Judge Ito became irate, threatening to stop TV coverage. Defense attorneys rescheduled to begin their opening statement tomorrow.

14

⚖️

O.J. on Trial

JUDGE ITO'S COURTROOM
JANUARY 24, 1995

Finally, opening statements. The endless legal skirmishing between the Dream Team and the prosecution had kept the jury out of the courtroom since January 18. Every day we'd come to the courthouse, and every day we'd head back to the hotel, bored and frustrated. But at last we'd been told, "Opening statements definitely begin today. The jury will be in the courtroom." Suddenly, the boredom disappeared. Adrenaline started pumping.

We were escorted into the jury box. Once again, all eyes were on us. We sat down, Judge Ito opened the proceedings. And finally, it was time for *The People v. O.J.*

Simpson. Judge Ito leaned back and spoke: "Mr. Darden."

Christopher Darden stood and began the prosecution's opening statement. It was devastating. First he, then Marcia Clark, presented the People's case. And the brutality of this double murder hit home in a way it never had before. Members of O.J.'s family, Nicole's family, and the Goldmans were present. I kept glancing at them, watching their reactions. I felt so sorry for them all. I felt sorry for O.J. I had made no judgments about his guilt or innocence. But for the first time, I heard the prosecution outline evidence that sounded overwhelming.

Then came the true horror. The photographs of that bloody murder scene. No one, except perhaps a law enforcement official or reporter who covers crime scenes, could look at those frightening photos without flinching. Everyone in that courtroom gasped. Family members sobbed, turned away, or reacted somehow. But inevitably, everyone forced themselves to look. Except O.J. Simpson. He *never* looked at the mutilated bodies of his ex-wife and Ron Goldman.

It was far gorier than I had expected. Yet I felt relieved in one respect: You could not see that Nicole's head had been nearly severed from her body. Thankfully, her hair covered that awful wound. But it was still horrible. Nicole was lying in blood that pooled out from her head and flowed down along her body. Such a huge amount of blood. It had drained down the condo walkway. Yet Nicole looked so still, almost peaceful, that if it weren't for the blood, you would have thought she was lying on her side asleep in her black halter dress. I looked across the courtroom at O.J. I'd been intent on the pictures, but I glanced at him several times. He still had not looked at his dead ex-wife.

Now there were photos of Ron Goldman. There was no illusion of peace here. Ron had been stabbed repeatedly. His body was mangled. He had dozens of stab wounds that you could see plainly because his shirt was pulled up.

Ron Goldman had died hard, boxed in and fighting desperately in a tiny area bounded by a gate and heavy shrubbery. His body lay sprawled helter-skelter, frozen in the last frenzied burst of energy he'd expended. Ron had been butchered. And a madman had done it. No question. Days later, I recalled that photo of Ron Goldman when the defense presented their theory that professional hit men had committed this crime. Not in my opinion. This didn't look like the work of a brutal professional. There was nothing methodical about it. This murder had passion and frenzy written all over it.

Everyone in America watched, heard, or read about what occurred on opening day. My purpose is not to recount a trial that has been publicly discussed and analyzed more than any other in history. But I truly think it was a case of "You had to be there" when Marcia Clark declared to the jury that the prosecution would present solid evidence of a blood trail leading directly from the victims to O.J.'s front door—and even into his bedroom. I will never forget the photo of those socks in O.J.'s bedroom.

Perhaps the TV cameras captured Marcia Clark's unshakable conviction and belief that she *knew* that she had the evidence that would prove O.J. was guilty of murder. But the impact of sitting right there, looking into her eyes as she spoke directly to the jury was overpowering—and a sobering moment for me as an African American. I know many white Americans find it hard to understand how we tend to have blind faith when one of our own is accused of a crime and the evidence is circumstantial. But there's a long, shameful history of black men being demonized and railroaded in criminal trials. We are skeptical of the white establishment, law enforcement officials, and the courts. And there's something else: We want so badly to be proud of our own.

But we're only human. It's difficult to convince us that a black man smart enough and talented enough to rise as high as O.J. Simpson could throw it all away on a crime of passion. But it's not *impossible* to convince us. Sitting there in that jury box, hearing Marcia Clark tell you with utter sincerity that she could prove *beyond a reasonable doubt* that O.J. did it, had tremendous impact. And it wasn't lost on the African-American jurors that Christopher Darden believed in O.J.'s guilt just as strongly. Let me say this right here and now: I'm not a fan of Marcia Clark or Darden. Both have shown open hostility toward me. But I never doubted their sincerity. And their impact on the jury on that opening day was devastating.

As the prosecution presented their case in court, I stole glances at my fellow jurors—especially the African Americans. I knew they were feeling what I was feeling. Somehow black folks had felt that this was all a put-up job—if not a conspiracy, then a rush to judgment by police and prosecutors eager for a quick conviction.

But something nagged at me as I sat in the jury box and listened to this promise of incriminating evidence to come. Months before, I'd watched TV coverage of O.J. both before and after his arrest. And like everyone in America, I'd seen the preliminary hearings, O.J.'s first days in court. And something struck me right away: O.J. looked like he was higher than a kite on drugs. And I don't mean prescription drugs!

How do I know? I've worked as a musician and I've known many people, some very close to me, who've been involved with drugs. I'd had a brief involvement myself as a young man. In short, I know what someone on drugs looks and acts like. And one of the first shocking whispers that spread through the black community after O.J.'s return from Chicago, and his subsequent arrest, was that he looked "high." I think journalists knew it too. There were accounts in the newspapers and on TV that said O.J. appeared to be "on medication," especially at Nicole's funeral.

I remember a conversation with a musician friend. "O.J. is high, man. And all this jive about prescription drugs is ridiculous," he said. "Have you seen him in the courtroom? Are people blind? He's strung out on something heavy. Look at the way he keeps pulling on his nose and rolling his eyes. He's not in control, man. He's suffering. O.J. is going through cold-turkey withdrawal right on national TV."

My wife picked up on O.J.'s condition and was shocked, yet sympathetic. "I hope they're treating him somehow and helping him get through this," she said. "Can't they see what's happening to that man?"

"You can bet that his jailers know, Beverly. But they don't care. Plenty of guys who go into the joint have drug problems and they just leave them in their cells to go cold turkey. Nobody holds their hands."

"Well, why don't they say something about it in the newspapers or on TV?"

"Beverly, I think most of the white journalists covering this trial don't know what a real junkie looks like. O.J. looks whacked out, but I guess his lawyers are just telling everyone that he's on medication. Hell, maybe they don't even know. And if they do, they're sure not going to talk about it to the press."

At the end of the day, after we heard the prosecution's opening statement, we went back to the hotel and right to dinner. I sat down with the other black jurors and realized immediately that everyone had been as deeply affected by what we'd heard in court as I had. I thought, Are we going to talk about this? I know we're not supposed to discuss the case among ourselves, but it's so hard to hold this in.

I glanced around the table at the faces of my fellow jurors. Some glances were exchanged, but no one said a word. The silence went on so long that I quietly looked at my watch and began timing how long it would last. Astounding as it may seem, no one at that table spoke for thirty minutes. Even more amazing was the completely different atmosphere at the table where the white and Latino jurors were seated. They were talking normally, routine dinner table talk and occasional laughter as someone cracked a joke.

I noted some angry glares from black jurors directed at the other table. But the contrast between the two groups was perfectly understandable, I thought. That first day of the trial had been solemn and eye-opening for all the jurors. Yet there were far deeper implications for black people in hearing for the first time that the prosecution had a strong case against O.J. Simpson. It's not racism. But it is about race. I hate racism, although I've been guilty of it from time to time. I imagine most people would make the same admission, if they were being honest. But there's nothing wrong with feeling a kinship and bond with other members of your ethnic group, religion, or nationality. For the black jurors, O.J. Simpson was one of our own. He was a brother, and he was in trouble. More than that, he was a black man who had risen high in a world that we still see as dominated by whites.

I know it's frustrating and difficult for white people to understand, but the deeply held belief in our community is that black men who rise high are eventually brought down by the white establishment; and that the police are quick to railroad black men. I believe that one reason polls have consistently shown that more blacks than whites believe O.J. is innocent is *not* that either side is necessarily being racist. It's that white people are looking at the available evidence and saying that when a wife is murdered, you look at the husband—while black people are reluctant to look closely at the evidence because it's too painful to contemplate that O.J.

is guilty, and they're sort of hoping that it will turn out to be just another police frame-up.

Our meal that night was one of the most painful ordeals I've ever gone through. Try to imagine hearing an astounding piece of news, then holding it in, and discussing it with no one. It literally makes you ache. Human nature is to share, to discuss, and plan. I'm no legal expert, but this aspect of our jury system is flawed. I think it goes against everything we believe as Americans to cut a jury off from hearing free speech by sequestering them. It's an unnatural situation.

If lawyers examine prospective jurors and choose them, why do judges think we're not competent enough to move freely in the community, then come into court and sit in the jury box to pass fair judgment on the evidence as it is presented? And I'm not just whining about the discomfort. It's strange and unnatural for human beings to be isolated and not allowed to talk about things weighing heavily on their minds. Tell the jury not to talk, by all means, but let them go home and lead normal lives.

I went into court and challenged an unfair

law suppressing freedom of speech—as guaranteed under the Constitution—to write this book. Judges attempt to exercise far too much control over the freedom of speech. Judge Ito himself was criticized, and I think rightly, for threatening to throw the TV cameras out of the courtroom on the first day of the trial because a cameraman had mistakenly shown one of the jurors for less than a second.

Judge Ito called the press "jackals" and tried to suppress certain journalists from speaking out. Yet he then went on television in Los Angeles for a five-part series on his life. I'm not trying to write a political tract. I'm just trying to show, through my experiences on the O.J. jury, how the jurors were subjected to emotional stresses that could have been avoided.

After that awful meal, I couldn't wait to phone Beverly. I was bursting to tell her . . . what? Like most married couples, my wife and I discuss everything. Yet I couldn't say a word. As usual, deputies were standing by to monitor our phone conversations.

"Hi, Beverly."

"Enjoying your vacation?"

"Not really."

"You had a big day in court, huh?"

"Beverly . . ."

"Oh, I forgot. You can't talk about it."

"That's right, Beverly. Man, I wish I was home playing with the kids. How is everybody?"

"Everybody's fine. Today I was out with Johnnie and a lady at the supermarket started saying how cute he was and then she asked me if he took after his daddy."

"Was this a white lady or a black lady?"

"Oh, it was a black lady. She wasn't being mean, just curious. She thought it was great that we were trying to adopt Johnnie."

"Well, I sure can't wait to see you all on Family Day. And I sure am looking forward to my conjugal visit."

"Well, I'll just bet you are," Beverly laughed.

"It's gonna be a whirlwind five hours, baby."

"Don't let your mouth promise what your tired old body can't deliver. You're pushing fifty, you know?"

"It's forty-seven, and right now I'm feeling like a very young forty-seven."

15 ⚖️
Pressure

Racism. Prejudice. Sexual jealousy. What was the first little rip in the social fabric of the O.J. jury? It came just moments after we learned we had been selected. All twenty-four of us were blowing off steam in the eleventh floor jury room, laughing and talking, caught up in the excitement of it all. It felt like graduation day, or being named to an all-star team. Now we were officially a page in the history books. And the first entry on that page was written when a fiftyish, heavy-set black woman suddenly cut through all the getting-to-know-you chatter by announcing: "By the way, guys . . . I'm gay."

Just like that. No preamble. Juror Num-

FAMILY SCRAPBOOK

(*Above*) Michael Knox, age 29

(*Left*) Former girlfriend Clare, a topless dancer at the TNT Club in San Diego, in a publicity photo.

(*Right*) Shocking photo of Harold Tolson after a brutal beating that nearly cost him his life—until Michael Knox intervened with a gun.

Photo by Thomas Knox

(Above) Michael with "my pride and joy," his 1957 Ford.

(Right) The author with former girlfriend Clare at the Kool Jazz Festival in San Diego, 1980.

(Below, L. to R.) Michael's 40th birthday party with family members Rodney, Pam, Sylvia and Deborah.

Michael and his wife Beverly at a 1991 New Year's Eve party.

On the job at the Federal Express depot in Marina del Rey, 1993.

(Above) At a birthday party for sister Deborah. (L. to R.) Family members Sylvia, Pam, Michael, Deborah, Thomas, and Cynthia.

(Left) Daughter Kimberly

(Below) Family picnic with Beverly, Trevon, and brother Thomas with his family, 1987.

THE PLAYERS

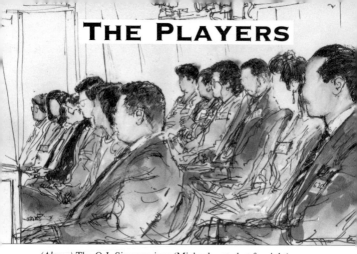

(Above) The O.J. Simpson jury (Michael seated at far right) as seen by veteran courtroom illustrator Bill Robles.

O.J. Simpson during a lighter moment in court *(left);* defense attorneys Johnnie Cochran *(middle),* Robert Shapiro *(above right),* and F. Lee Bailey *(right).*

All trial and juror photos: AP/Wide World Photos

Judge Lance Ito

Prosecutor Marcia Clark with defense attorney Robert Blasier.

Ex-Jurors

(Above) Tracy "T.K." Kennedy gives his version of why Judge Ito dismissed him from the jury.

(Above right) Jeanette Harris (at left) prepares to drop her bombshell on KCAL-TV after her dismissal.

(Right) A distraught Tracy Hampton in front of her home the day she was dismissed.

ber 23's declaration of sexual preference came whizzing out of the blue. Why she chose that moment—or why she said it at all—is a mystery. It was the kind of confidence you might be drawn into sharing with a small group of intimate friends. Not with twenty-three total strangers.

For just the tiniest fraction of a second, everybody froze. Conversation skipped half a heartbeat, then raced on again in high gear. For a moment, I thought my imagination was playing tricks. I shot a quick glance at Juror Number 23, whose name was Sarah, and caught a fleeting look of bewilderment on her face as she realized no one was going to acknowledge her statement. I remember feeling bewildered and somewhat ashamed. It seemed heartless not to say something. Everyone just kept talking, acting as if they hadn't heard a word. Yet I knew they had. I was standing further away from her than several of the other jurors.

From that day on, Juror Number 23 was ostracized by some of the black female jurors. It wasn't overt. It wasn't that nobody spoke to her. But there was always a coolness, a reserve. And remarks were passed when her female lover arrived for conjugal visits. All because of two little words: "I'm gay."

Human beings are funny animals. Lock twenty-four of us in a room and give us all the same skin color, and we'll start discriminating on the basis of hair color. Give us all the same hair color and the people who wear glasses will snub the people who don't. Prejudices go on and on and on. And that's just how it went with the O.J. jury.

The first really ugly rift occurred when Tracy Hampton, the twenty-six-year-old airline stewardess, decided to switch tables and eat with the black jurors, at the table where I sat. Previously she'd been sitting with the alternate jurors. It was a mistake. The older females at our table—Lisa, Millie, Pamela, and especially Jeanette Harris—bristled almost visibly when Tracy first joined us. Why? It seemed to stem from nothing more than jealousy. Tracy was young and extremely attractive. She was polite, nice, and made every effort to defer to the older women. Yet every effort she made to be friendly was firmly rebuffed. Worse than that, they eventually ostracized her completely.

I picked up on what was happening immediately. Strangely enough, it took awhile for Tracy to realize she was being shunned, totally. It sounds incredible, but Tracy is so shy and naive—and apparently far less emotionally developed than her years—that some things just sailed right over her head.

Gradually, it dawned on Tracy that none of the other women at the table ever spoke to her. And even when she asked them direct questions, they responded by acting as if they hadn't heard her. Even worse, they never looked directly at her. It was brutal. Then I did something that made the situation even worse. Attempting to fill the void of some of the uncomfortable silences, I started speaking to Tracy more and more. It's amazing how dumb men can be in these intricate social situations. Naturally, the more attention I paid to Tracy, the more the other women resented her and shut her out. And as Tracy became more sensitive to her isolation, the more she turned to me as someone she could confide in.

Every night after dinner, Tracy would seek me out. We'd sit at a small table in the lounge, out of earshot from the other jurors.

"What am I going to do, Michael?" she'd say. "I've tried everything. I smile, I laugh at their jokes, I agree with everything they say. Now they won't even look at me. They talk around me as if I wasn't even there. I hate this, Michael. I can't stand it anymore."

Tracy started to cry.

I reached over and patted her hand. I felt uncomfortable, helpless. What could I say to her? We kept having the same conversation over and over. As sorry as I felt for her, I sometimes felt like I just wanted to escape, avoid getting enmeshed in her problems. But I felt so sorry for her. Even if I couldn't suggest a solution to this nasty situation, I could at least be sympathetic and keep her company.

I told her, "Tracy, it's almost like the harder you try, the worse it gets. I think if you could just ignore them, pretend that you don't care and stop talking to them so much, you'd do better. I know that sounds crazy to you, but look at our lesbian friend. They try to give her the cold shoulder, but she acts like she doesn't even notice it and just keeps on talking. And if one of them doesn't answer her, she just gets right in their face and makes them pay attention. They don't mess with her."

Tracy, her hands twisting nervously in her lap, looked at me, her eyes filled with tears.

"Michael, I can't be like her. She's . . . different. They're all so different from me."

How right she was. In addition to all her other "problems," Tracy sounded and even acted like a white girl. She was what I call "bourgeois black." Most of the older black female jurors were girls from the 'hood, women more connected to their ethnic roots. I'd seen it before. African Americans who move up the socioeconomic scale seemingly get whacked from both sides—they're not quite white, but they're not exactly black anymore, either.

"I want to go home, Michael!"

"Now, Tracy . . ."

She was sobbing. "Please, Michael, tell me what to do. How can I get out of here?"

Oh, man. One part of me wanted desperately to help Tracy, who reminded me so much of my sister Deborah. Not in her character, but because she had lost what I'll call her "street smarts." It had been the same with my sister. Deborah had pursued higher education and has a master's degree in health sciences. The way she talked, I used to joke that no one would ever guess that we were brother and sister. I think I'm reasonably well spoken and articulate, but I'm more "ethnic" than my sister.

And that's not to imply that Jeanette Harris, for instance, is not well educated. Jeanette has a college degree and, as millions of TV viewers saw after she was removed from the jury, her skill at communicating is excellent.

Tracy said, "Michael, do you think I should go to Judge Ito? Do you think he'd let me go home?"

I sighed. It was the same conversation we always had. How could I help her? How do you tell someone that their shyness and paranoia—Tracy's fear that male deputies were spying on her, for example—made them a born victim? I hated myself for feeling that way, but at the time I felt there was nothing I could do. In light of what eventually happened to Tracy, I wish I'd tried to be more helpful.

"Tracy, you've got to calm down. You've just got to. Now go to bed. You look very tired. Just stop thinking about all this."

After a few more tears, Tracy got up like an obedient child and went off to her room.

The very next day, everything came to a head. It was an ugly scene. During the morning meal, all of us were having a general discussion about some topic. I can't recall what it was, but in a moment of silence Tracy asked a question. I think she was probably trying to take my advice about getting "right in the faces" of the older women, and she virtually demanded an answer. It didn't work. In the silence, no one responded to Tracy. The women ignored her completely. I was just about to open my mouth and cover up the embarrassing silence as usual, when Tracy suddenly bolted from the table, crying her eyes out. She ran out onto a patio off the dining room and sat there alone, literally shaking with sobs. No one at the table made a move or said a word. Angrily, I slammed my fork down, pushed my chair back, and walked out onto the patio.

"Tracy, don't cry . . . you just can't let them get to you this way . . ."

She could barely speak the words, she was sobbing so hard. But I'll never forget what she said.

"Michael, I want to go home . . . none of these people here are like me. They don't come from where I come from."

Man, I was furious! How could these people be so cruel to one of their own? Tracy wouldn't come in, so I left her out on the patio and walked back inside. I confronted the women—including Jeanette, Lisa, Millie, Pamela, and Sarah, the lesbian juror—and said: "Could you guys please let up on this girl? It's making all of us uncomfortable and I don't think there's any reason for it. Couldn't you just please try to be a little more gentle and accepting? I think this is a sisterhood thing. You're all black women and you should let Tracy into the group. She wants so badly for you guys to like her."

Jeanette gave me one of her stony looks. She just stared at me and said nothing. The others avoided my gaze. For a moment I thought I was going to get the total cold shoulder. Then Lisa snapped: "She's a big girl. She should be able to deal with whatever she has to deal with all by herself."

Man, this was cold! I searched around in my mind for something that would persuade these women to lighten up. Then Millie got up, without a word and walked out to the patio. For a moment, I thought she was going to read Tracy out, give her hell. But after a moment, even though I couldn't hear the words, it was plain to see that Millie was consoling Tracy. She sat out there with the sobbing girl and calmed her down. Then Millie led Tracy back into the room and sat her down at the table. I waited hopefully, thinking Millie might say a few words to promote future peace and harmony. She didn't, and nothing more was said at the table that day.

Looking back on it today, I think the seeds of the O.J. jury revolt were sown right there and then. Cliques were forming and re-forming, pressure was building and the manipulation was beginning. As I sat there that day, finishing that cold meal, I glanced over at Jeanette Harris. I expected to see anger and annoyance because Millie had brought Tracy back into the fold. What I saw instead puzzled me. Jeanette actually looked happily content, as if she were savoring the most delicious meal she had ever eaten.

16 ♎

Conjugal Night

JANUARY 28, 1995

Anticipation. The most powerful aphrodisiac known to man. It was whipping some of us into a frenzy that Saturday. I tried to remember the raunchier lyrics to an old rhythm and blues song that starts out, "Well, it's Saturday night and I just got paid . . ." I'd learned it back when I was a young musician. But all I could recall was that the next line ended with "laid."

There's an old song that says, "Saturday night is the loneliest night of the week . . ." Not this Saturday night! No, sir. After nearly two weeks of being caged, this tiger was ready to roar. Tonight was the big night. Our first conjugal visit.

You could literally feel the excitement. Some of the jurors tried to hide it, but it was there. We'd all had a bellyful of this isolation. We wanted desperately to see our loved ones face-to-face. And we were looking forward to some good old S-E-X.

Anticipation. You could actually see it. People were smiling a lot, talking a little faster, making quick little movements with their hands and eyes as they conversed. Nervous energy crackled. The women would giggle sharply, then look around and lower their eyes. And every remark seemed to take on a double meaning. I'd say something like: "Hey, Fred, why are you all dressed up today in that fine new shirt? This isn't Sunday. You're looking sharp, man!"

Then he'd say something like, "Well, I'm feeling sharp . . . mighty sharp." Then all the men would laugh gruffly. There were some funny cracks, but nothing really blue.

Not all the jurors had a spouse or partner coming for Conjugal Night. I felt happy for Lisa, who'd pushed the hardest for getting these visits. Unfortunately, her husband was in the navy and overseas. Millie and Lisa, my two best pals on the jury, would be alone that night. I sensed disappointment among those for whom this wouldn't be a special time. But even they got caught up in the enthusiasm and excitement. There was a festive air all day long at meals, in the lounge, and the video room. Even the deputies caught the spirit. They seemed friendlier, looser. I had a sneaky feeling Judge Ito had told them to lighten up for this special occasion.

A few days before, the head deputy, Deputy Jex, a big, well-built black man with a no-nonsense air of authority and dignity, had told us how the conjugal visits would work. He explained the procedure in that funny, stilted language only cops seem to speak. It sounded something like this: "The conjugal visits will commence at seven o'clock and will have a duration of no more than five hours, ending promptly at twelve midnight. To effect the transportation schedule necessary to meet these requirements, your visitors must be present at the courthouse no later than 5:30 P.M. At that time, deputies will shuttle the visitors here to the hotel. You may greet and spend time with your visitors in

153

any of the common areas, such as the lounge, or video room . . ."

That got a big chuckle from everybody. I said to somebody sitting next to me, "Man, I'd just like to see the look on Beverly's face if I told her, 'Hey, baby, good to see you. Let's go hang out in the video room for a few hours.' "

Deputy Jex droned on: ". . . but for those of you who would prefer to receive your visitors in your rooms . . ."

That got a big laugh. I never did figure out whether Deputy Jex knew he was going to get laughs with those lines. He never cracked a smile. But I suspect that underneath that badge beat the heart of a closet comedian.

The explanation of the rules droned on. On the O.J. jury, somebody was always spouting a rule at you. And our visitors were going to get their own speech on the rules. They'd be told that conjugal visits were a privilege; that visitors must pledge never to reveal the location of the hotel, must not engage in conversation with any juror except the one they were visiting, must not attempt to discuss the case during the conjugal visit, blah, blah, blah . . .

This would be the first time any of us would be absolutely alone with another human being without a deputy around to monitor our conversation. I thought, Beverly is almost certain to ask me questions about the case. It's only natural. But I wonder if they'd go so far as to bug our rooms?

I decided I was getting paranoid. But I made a mental note not to assume that Beverly and I would have total privacy . . . just in case.

The jurors had another treat in store. After the conjugal visit on Saturday, Sunday would be Family Day. Any member of our family—mother, father, brothers, sisters, uncles, cousins, grandparents, and, of course, our wives and kids—would meet us at the courthouse on Sunday. They would not be allowed to come to the jurors' hotel, for security reasons. But there'd be a great catered meal. It was going to be one great weekend. Even the jurors who didn't have partners coming for conjugal visits on Saturday night could look forward to seeing family members on Sunday.

One sad note. Poor Tracy Hampton looked very upset. She'd be alone on this conjugal night. And she was still depressed over her shunning by the older black female jurors. A conjugal visit wouldn't have solved her problems, but it would have helped.

Tracy had confided in me about the man in her life. She said he was older and wealthy. He was very generous, always giving her gifts. I sat and talked with her for awhile.

"Why didn't you ask him to be here with you, Tracy?"

"You don't understand, Michael. We're not . . . you know, intimate yet."

"Oh, I'm sorry. I didn't mean to pry or anything."

"I know you don't."

"But I just felt so sorry that you're all down and everything . . ."

The minute I said it, I wished that I hadn't. Tears sprang into her eyes. Now I'd made her feel worse.

"Uh, Tracy, uh . . . I just wanted to . . ."

Tracy stood up quickly. "It's getting late. I think I'll turn in now. Good night, Michael. I know you'll have a very pleasant evening."

Tracy walked off quickly. I caught the eye of one of the other male jurors. I think it was Carl. The look we exchanged was pure communication between two men. It said, what a shame that such a fine young woman is destined to be alone on this night of all nights.

One part of me was glad that Tracy had terminated our conversation so abruptly. Nothing I said or did could ease her troubles. And I had to be up, in more ways than one, for my first night with Beverly in nearly two weeks.

I looked at the clock. It was nearly time for our visitors to arrive. I elected to wait in my room for Beverly. I thought she'd feel too self-conscious walking in and greeting me in front of strangers. It's really weird when you think of it. How many times are you in a situation where you look at two people and absolutely know that they're going to be whooping it up in bed moments later? I got up from where I was sitting in the lounge, stretched, and said as casually as I could: "Well . . . I guess it's about that time."

There was a chorus of "Good nights" and one "You got that right!"

I walked down the corridor, and as I passed the last deputy guard post, one of the male deputies grinned and said, "Turning in early tonight, huh?"

I winked. "Yeah, I just can't keep my eyes open a minute longer."

In my room, I brushed my teeth for about the tenth time that day. Then I brushed my hair. I had only done that about forty or fifty times. Finally, there was nothing to do but wait. I looked out the window at the lights of Los Angeles for awhile. With no TV or telephone in the room, looking out the window was something I did a lot, believe it or not. One thing about sequestration, it gives you a lot of time to think. Too much time.

There was a knock at the door. I walked over and opened it and there was Beverly. I said thanks to the deputy who escorted her. I pulled Beverly inside, closed the door and took her in my arms, smothering her with kisses. After a minute, we came up for air and she said, "Can you slow down a minute so I can take a look at this room?"

"Baby, I sure missed you. You are looking gorgeous."

Beverly was checking out my current "home."

"This is a nice hotel, Michael," she said. She walked over and looked out the window. "I had no idea you were staying at this hotel. I didn't think they'd be putting you up in a place as classy as this."

"Oh, baby, I guess it's O.K. But it's getting pretty old, I'll tell ya. Damn, you are looking beautiful. Did you lose some weight, or something?"

"Yeah, I'm so lonesome for you I haven't been able to eat a thing—I wish," she laughed. "Actually, I had my hair done. Do you like it?"

"Yeah, I like it. Man, I can't believe you're here."

"Well, believe it," she said. "Courtesy of the sheriff's department. It sure is weird being carried over here and walked up to your hotel room like this. I feel like I'm some kind of call girl."

"Hold that thought, baby. That sounds like one of those fantasy things they say will put the spice back in a marriage."

"Fine with me, mister," she joked as I reached for her again. "You just put the money up there on the dresser before we get down to business." I talked her into trusting me until payday.

For a long time after that, we didn't say much of anything. Later, lying in bed with the lights out, Beverly said: "Well, we're just going to have to sequester you more often."

We both started laughing like fools. After awhile, we started to talk. Man, it felt good to just open up with someone you trusted. Beverly finally asked about the trial and how it was going. And did I think O.J. was guilty? I got very serious and told her we absolutely could not talk about the trial. Then I whispered about my paranoia that the room might be bugged. Beverly started laughing again. I got a little annoyed. I admitted I was probably being overcautious, but that bugging was possible. Beverly was laughing so hard she was almost gasping for breath.

"Can you just imagine? . . . Judge Ito listening to the tapes of everything that's going on in these rooms tonight . . ." Now she had me laughing uncontrollably too. Later, I told her about some of the things that had been going on. When I mentioned the ostracism of Tracy Hampton and of the lesbian juror, Beverly said: "That isn't right. Black people are always complaining about prejudice from white people. And then we go and act that way toward each other. It just isn't right."

While we were talking, there were some sudden loud bangs on the door. "What the hell . . ." I said as I switched on the light and looked at my watch. "It can't be the deputies. It's not time for you to go yet. It's nowhere near midnight."

There were another couple of bangs on the door and I heard some giggling. Female voices. Then I guessed who it was. "It's just a couple of the female jurors who don't have partners coming to see them tonight," I told Beverly. "It's Millie and Lisa joking around.

They're two of the good people on this jury."

Beverly was not amused. "Just how friendly are these women, running around and banging on your door in the middle of the night when you're with your wife?" Beverly snapped.

"Oh, they're just keyed up with all the excitement, baby. And they jog up and down these long corridors every night for exercise," I said. Beverly looked exasperated. "You people really are going crazy in here," she said.

"Oh now, baby, you need to calm down," I said, reaching for her again.

Promptly at midnight, there was another knock. A deputy shouted through the door that the vans would be leaving soon and all visitors should assemble in the hallway. Beverly was all dressed and ready to go. I kissed her again, then opened the door, and we walked out into the corridor.

It was like lover's lane out there! Everyone was grinning and looking a little embarrassed. One thing that raised a lot of eyebrows was Sarah, the lesbian juror, arm in arm with her female lover who was dressed in a man's suit and shoes. The next day there was a lot of whispering and gossiping among the jurors about her. Weeks later, after she'd shown up for several conjugal visits, I remember the big juror, Fred, saying snidely: "That woman's got more tailor-made suits than I have."

Just before Beverly left that night I kissed her and said, "Five hours just isn't long enough. But at least I'll see you tomorrow. I sure am looking forward to seeing our kids."

17

⚖️

Family Day

JANUARY 29, 1995

Racism. It sneaked up and blindsided me when I wasn't looking. Who would expect the ugliness of racial hatred on Family Day?

All America heard Jeanette Harris make her sensational claims of racial bias toward black jurors by white jurors and white deputies. She titillated us with her lurid tale of a white woman who physically assaulted Jeanette and a large black male. News accounts at the time reported that Judge Ito commented during his investigation of the juror revolt, after hearing Jeanette's claims, that the idea of a woman physically intimidating a big man just didn't compute.

The woman Jeanette had accused, Francine Florio-Bunten, was removed from the jury on May 25, 1995, and totally denied the claim that she'd hit anybody.

One white friend of mine joked that Jeanette's comments conjured up images of white deputies strolling around the hotel and jury room slapping billy clubs in their hands and calling me "Boy." Well, let me set the record straight: Everything I'm reporting is based on personal observation and my opinion. But as far as I know, there were no incidents of racism in the first couple of weeks that the O.J. jurors were sequestered.

Obviously, that first separation of the jurors in the dining room, when they sat at tables according to their skin color, had a racial dimension. And that could have qualified as racism if, for example, the deputies had reserved the "best" table for the white jurors and ordered us to segregate. And Tracy Hampton's shunning by the older black female jurors had perhaps a hint of black-on-black racism sometimes aimed at blacks who'd "gone uptown" and were "acting white." But I think it was more a case of female jealousy.

No question, the O.J. jury was an ethnic tinder box. The fuse was lit. And on Family Day, of all days, the first overt incident of racism I know about was about to explode—in *my* face!

When we got to the courthouse that Sunday, I staked out a spot in the corner of the large visiting room assigned to us. I wanted to keep my family somewhat away from the other jurors because I have four boisterous boys. Darnell is eight, Reynaldo is five, Manuel is three, and little Johnnie is just fifteen months, but he's already quite a handful. They're not bad kids or abnormally noisy. I just wanted to make sure that Beverly and I could keep them under control. I didn't want to disturb the peace and quiet of anybody's visit with family and friends.

Finally, Beverly and the boys arrived. After a few moments of excitement and affection, with the boys yelling "Daddy, Daddy!" and jumping all over me, I hustled everybody over to the little area I had staked out. I told the kids we'd be having some great things to eat later and things calmed down a bit.

The older boys started playing some game they had brought with them and were actually pretty quiet. And I held little baby Johnnie on my lap. Now I'm not what you'd call a self-conscious person. I'm outgoing and I like people. So I'm not the kind of guy who walks into a gathering and immediately starts worrying about what people think of him. Beverly, on the other hand, is the kind of woman who observes everything and misses nothing. I pick up a lot of signals from her in social situations, the way many husbands do; like when she's telling me I'm talking too much, or I shouldn't order another drink.

Now I sensed something from Beverly. I looked around the visiting room. A lot of eyes were staring our way. And some of them flashed pure hatred. I knew why, instantly. My wife and I are foster parents. The foster children consist of two Hispanic boys, one black boy, and our white infant, little Johnnie. So we're used to getting odd looks when we're out with our mixed brood. Usually, people of all races find little Johnnie, who has blond hair and blue eyes, absolutely

167

adorable. Not this time! A few of the jurors dropped over to say hello, but most of the black jurors made their disapproval plain. Not only didn't they come over to meet my wife and say hello, they kept shooting us dirty looks. The worst of these was Mr. Johnson. He glared at me with pure hatred.

This was amazing. It wasn't that Mr. Johnson disliked me. We'd gotten along well so far, and I'd always found him to be an upstanding older man, worthy of dignity and respect. He and I had enjoyed some very cordial conversations. This new reaction was a shock. Beverly, who gets very angry in situations like this, hissed: "Who is that old man, Michael? Why does he keep glaring at us like that?"

Now I was getting angry. I started to hand her baby Johnnie and said, "What the hell does that old man think he's playing at? I'm going to talk to him."

Beverly pushed little Johnnie back into my lap. "Don't say anything, Michael. You're not going to change his mind or anybody's mind. We've just got this little bit of time for you and the kids to see each other, so don't let them ruin it for us." Beverly shook her head angrily. "How could anyone hate someone for loving little children?"

I calmed down. It was an effort, but Beverly was right. And ironically, before the end of the visitation, *all* of the white jurors came by to say hello. But only three or four of the black jurors did. And those evil looks from Johnson never stopped. I knew there'd be trouble ahead from him. It was another one of those moments when I cursed the day I'd ever joined the O.J. jury. It wouldn't be the last.

Another note about Family Day: It turned out that the lesbian juror had children of her own. They were grown up, a son and a daughter who had children of their own. So Sarah was a grandmother. Her whole extended family showed up on Family Day, and her female lover was there too. Everybody kept watching to see what the interaction would be between Sarah's lover and her grown children. And I think all the looky-loos got a big surprise. Sarah's children and grandchildren accepted her lover like she was part of the family. And that seemed to irritate the hell out of the jurors who'd ostracized Juror Number 23 from the beginning.

The last thing Beverly said to me that day was: "I never realized how intolerant some black people can be. I just never noticed it like this before. Maybe it's that being sequestered is bringing out the worst in people. Don't let them get to you, Michael."

18 ⚖ Trial Chronology

JANUARY 25–FEBRUARY 7, 1995

Wednesday
January 25, 1995

15th day of sequestration
Jury present

•   Judge Ito declared that the Court TV camera could remain in the courtroom.

•   Johnnie Cochran began the opening statements for the defense. He said O.J. Simpson is "an innocent man wrongly accused." Cochran characterized the police investigation as sloppy, and that the investigation against O.J. was a "rush to judgment."

• O.J. showed the jury the football injuries to his knees, and also displayed his hands.

Jury not in court

• Out of the jury's presence, prosecutor William Hodgman angrily accused the defense team of violating discovery rules by failing to turn over witnesses' names before opening statements.

Out of court

• At a late meeting of the prosecution team in the district attorney's office, William Hodgman was stricken with chest pains and rushed to a hospital.

Thursday
January 26, 1995

16th day of sequestration
Jury not present

• Judge Ito cancelled the regular session of the trial for Thursday and Friday.

• The court was occupied by a day-long hearing regarding possible sanctions against the defense for failure to turn over witness statements and other items to the prosecution in a timely manner.

• Prosecutors accused the defense of referring in opening statements to the expected testimony of defense witnesses even though prosecutors had not been given their statements.

• Prosecutor Darden denounced the proposed defense witnesses as "heroin addicts, thieves, felons and . . . the only person I have ever known to be a court-certified pathological liar." He stated that prospective defense witness Mary Anne Gerchas owed $23,000 to the J.W. Marriott Corp. "We know she had nine lawsuits pending in the D.A.'s office. In our bad check section there are approximately $10,000 in bad checks that relate to this person."

Saturday
January 28, 1995

18th day of sequestration

Sunday
January 29, 1995

19th day of sequestration

Monday
January 30, 1995

20th day of sequestration
Jury present

• Judge Ito ruled that as a sanction to the defense for failure to comply with the rules of discovery, the prosecution would be given the opportunity to make additional opening statements. He instructed jurors that Johnnie Cochran had violated the law when he failed to provide the prosecution with the witness statements.

- Johnnie Cochran concluded his opening remarks, criticizing the quality of the prosecution evidence-gathering as slipshod, resulting in contamination.

Tuesday
January 31, 1995

21st day of sequestration
Jury present

- In an unusual ruling by Judge Ito, prosecutor Marcia Clark was granted ten minutes to reopen her opening statements. She called prospective defense witness Mary Anne Gerchas a "known liar" and a "Simpson case groupie."

- The prosecution opened with testimony from witnesses detailing a 1989 spousal battery call at the O.J. Simpson Brentwood estate. Sharyn Gilbert, the 911 operator, Detective Mike Farrell, and Detective John Edwards testified.

Wednesday
February 1, 1995

22nd day of sequestration
Jury present

• Judge Ito, after hearing arguments from both sides regarding the admissibility of proposed testimony by witness Ronald Shipp, ruled for the prosecution. Ronald Shipp took the stand.

• Shipp was questioned by Christopher Darden. Carl Douglas conducted the cross-examination for the defense.

Thursday
February 2, 1995

23rd day of sequestration
Jury present

• Ron Shipp continued on the stand, cross-examined by Carl Douglas for the defense.

- Michael Stevens took the stand for the prosecution. He is the senior D.A. investigator who opened the safe-deposit box of Nicole Brown Simpson to reveal photos of her with bruises. Also in the safe were other items, including a handwritten letter of apology from O.J. Simpson.

- Tape of an October 25, 1993, call to 911 was played. Witness Terri Moore, the 911 operator, testified she had received the call from Nicole.

- Robert Lerner, the LAPD officer who responded to Nicole Simpson's 911 call, testified for the prosecution.

Outside of court

- Judge Ito met with L.A. County Sheriff's deputies who were part of an investigation into possible misconduct of jury members.

Friday
February 3, 1995

24th day of sequestration
Jury present

• Catherine Boe lived next door to Nicole in 1992. She testified for the prosecution about domestic incidents to which she was a witness.

• Carl Colby, Boe's husband, testified to seeing someone looking into Nicole's house late at night. He called 911, thinking it was a burglar. It turned out to be O.J.

• Denise Brown, look-alike sister of Nicole, testified to incidents of physical abuse by O.J. She testified for approximately twenty minutes before breaking down.

Jury not present

• Rockne Harmon, prosecution DNA expert, challenged remarks from the defense's opening statement regarding blood evidence on a pair of socks found in O.J.'s bedroom.

• Robert Blaiser, a DNA expert for the defense, disagreed with prosecution allegations.

Saturday
February 4, 1995

25th day of sequestration

Sunday
February 5, 1995

26th day of sequestration

Monday
February 6, 1995

27th day of sequestration
Jury present

• Denise Brown concluded her testimony for the prosecution and was cross-examined by Robert Shapiro.

• Candace Garvey, wife of former baseball player, Steve Garvey, and a friend of Nicole's, testified for the prosecution about O.J. Simpson's behavior at Sydney Simpson's dance recital.

• Cynthia Shahian, a friend of Nicole's, testified about a letter O.J. Simpson sent Nicole in June threatening to turn her in to the IRS.

Tuesday
February 7, 1995

28th day of sequestration
Jury present

• Another juror was removed by Judge Ito. A sixty-three-year-old retired legal secretary was replaced by a fifty-four-year-old postal worker.

- Stewart Tanner, a bartender at Mezzaluna, testified for the prosecution about the last known activities of Ron Goldman.

- Pablo Fenjves, a neighbor of Nicole's, testified he heard a dog's wailing between 10:15 and 10:20 P.M. the night of the killings.

- Kimberly Goldman, sister of victim Ron Goldman, testified, identifying work clothes found in her brother's apartment after his death.

- Tia Gavin and Karen Crawford, Mezzaluna employees, testified about the last time they saw Ron Goldman.

Jury not present

- Defense attorney Johnnie Cochran complained about the small angel pin that Marcia Clark was wearing. Judge Ito reserved judgment on that issue.

19 ⚖️ Tension

Finally the pace of the O.J. Simpson trial was picking up. After endless legal skirmishing and stop-and-start opening statements, the proceedings lurched forward and settled into a snail-like, but steady pace.

One of the first witnesses to take the stand was the very creepy ex-LAPD officer Ron Shipp. He came across as a drunk and a leech who had deluded himself into thinking he was O.J. Simpson's best buddy. What a punk! He had admitted drug problems and had been more or less booted off the police force. He confirmed he was in the process of writing a book. Shipp saw himself as the guy who was going to "nail O.J." This was some of the first testimony from a witness that I'd heard, so I took it very seriously. I tried to gauge how I would weigh Shipp's testimony against my feeling that he was a pathetic excuse for a human being. I decided that I didn't necessarily disbelieve his testimony. Even though he was a loser, he didn't strike me as an out-and-out liar.

A puzzling part of Shipp's testimony, to me anyway, was his claim that O.J. told him after the murders that he had experienced dreams about killing Nicole. On this point, I felt Shipp was telling the truth. But I couldn't figure out for the life of me, why anyone who was a potential suspect in a murder case would freely admit to dreams about killing one of the victims. Today I'm a little more sophisticated—or at least I've talked to lawyers and journalists who know how things work from the inside. It has been suggested to me that one of O.J.'s lawyers or cop pals might have tipped him that one of the ways to explain a "guilty" reading on a lie detector test is to first stipulate that you have had dreams about committing the crime.

If, for instance, O.J. had taken a lie detector test and answered "no" to the question, "Did you kill Nicole?" and the lie detector registered a "yes" answer, it could be argued that the dream of a murder had caused the machine to register a false result. Interesting theory, but my guess is that the jury didn't give much significance to the dream testimony. If it was some kind of ploy dreamed up by O.J. and/or his legal experts, it didn't score.

By now, you're probably wondering why I don't know what the jury was saying behind the scenes—about the Ron Shipp dream testimony, or all the other testimony, for that matter. Today, people still say to me, "You guys really did discuss the trial when you got back to the hotel, didn't you? I've heard lawyers on TV say that they're sure the jurors discuss everything. And after Jeanette Harris came off the jury, she said you guys discussed the trial. True or not true?"

Here's a bombshell revelation for the so-called "O.J. experts": Jeanette Harris flat-out *lied* when she said the jury discussed the trial! I never heard any juror—Jeanette included—say one word about testimony or about O.J. himself!

Judge Ito had warned over and over that we must NEVER discuss the trial. No one ever broke that rule, to my knowledge. Why Jeanette uttered such an outrageous lie and dishonored us all still puzzles me. In my opinion, Jeanette is manipulative, even malevolent. But I never believed she was stupid. Whatever her reason for making that statement, she later backed off it after her first TV interview. When Judge Ito called her back to court after her television debut, I'm sure he shocked all the jurors by telling them that Jeanette had painted them as irresponsible jurors.

You won't hear any sensational revelations from me about secret conversations among the jurors because the O.J. jurors never broke that rule. But keeping our mouths shut got painful. The fact that we were never able to discuss the biggest thing in our lives at that moment—added to our isolation from family, friends, workplaces, radio, uncensored newspapers, and TV—

made us all a little loopy. Nutty jurors don't help a trial and that's the key to the so-called "jury revolt" against Judge Ito.

When you're locked down like we were, the tiniest annoyances can become huge irritations. Take Carl's bad breath, for example. Some of us used to joke that Carl had "hellacious halitosis." I'm not talking the puny kind of unpleasant breath you sometimes get a whiff of when someone hasn't brushed their teeth. People actually complained that they hated mealtimes with Carl because his bad breath would hit you even from the other side of the table. Or he would sit in the lounge or video room and a foul, funky odor would ooze up like a cloud.

All of us made jokes about it. I remember one day when somebody who'd just experienced an odor encounter with Carl said, "Man, he has some ass-kicking breath!" Every time Carl got near, I'd get up and leave, and I'm sure he knew why. But Tracy Hampton, who was probably the world's most polite woman, would sit there and tolerate him if he suddenly joined her.

Carl hung around Tracy a lot. He was

very attracted to her. And that gave him two reasons for disliking me: I hated his bad breath and didn't make any bones about it; and Tracy always gravitated toward me because she'd come to see me as her one true friend on the jury.

I think Carl knew we joked about his bad breath. Lisa and Millie were always making cracks and one night, when they were jogging up and down the hotel corridors, they came up with the idea of buying a big bottle of Listerine and putting it outside Carl's door. They came to me with their plan and I'll admit it cracked me up. But I told them it wasn't a good idea. All of us were under pressure and a practical joke like that might cause bad blood. After that, though, all any of us had to do to get a laugh was to whisper "Listerine" whenever Carl passed by.

Little things became big deals. People's tempers were frayed. One day I happened to mention to Tracy Hampton that I could really use a manicure.

"I'll do your nails, Michael. I'll do them tonight after dinner."

"Oh no, Tracy, I wouldn't dream of asking you to do that."

"I'm really good at it and I don't mind at all. I like doing nails. It's fun. And it'll give me something to do. I'm so sick of watching videos."

That evening Tracy did my nails. Right away, evil looks started. And again, it was black jurors. White jurors would walk by and either smile absentmindedly, or say something like, "Hey, can I be next?" I thought Carl was going to have a heart attack on the spot. This man had a bad case of the hots for Tracy. Mr. Johnson shot us some angry stares, but that didn't spring from jealousy. He just flat hated me.

The reaction from some older female jurors was different yet again. Through body language and raised eyebrows, they telegraphed their suspicion that Tracy and I were involved in a budding romance. Nothing could be further from the truth. I'm as susceptible to a pretty girl as the next man, but Tracy was just a pal. Period! It bothered me that people would think that. There were troublemaking snitches on this jury—and the last thing a married man needs is somebody spreading false rumors that he's involved with another woman.

Once again, let me offer proof that I'm not exaggerating: Right after Tracy Hampton left the jury and was rushed to the hospital— and shortly before this book was completed—major news organizations in the United States and overseas contacted me to ask if Tracy was pregnant with my child. They quoted "sources close to the case."

First of all, under conditions of around-the-clock supervision by as many as ten deputies, anyone who could secretly do what's necessary to achieve a pregnancy would have to be a magician. And here's a question: Who do you think the media's "sources close to the case" might be? It's possible, but highly unlikely, that it's someone still sitting on the jury. Or it could be a deputy. And could it be someone who was released from the jury and doesn't like me or Tracy Hampton? Any guesses?

The night I sat there with Tracy doing my

nails, I made a mental note to stop associating with her so much. Then I said to myself, that's ridiculous. Why should I react to a few people with nasty thoughts? And there aren't that many pleasant people around here to talk to.

I still couldn't help feeling sorry for Tracy. She was trying desperately to curry favor with the other women, but without much success. Poor Tracy. I felt like she was a kid sister. As I've said before, she reminds me very much of my own sister Deborah. I felt protective towards her. Tracy's situation wasn't helped by the fact that she had her phobia about being spied on by the white male deputies. Later, she'd accuse a white female deputy of coming into her room while she was sleeping. Tracy complained to Deputy Jex, the head deputy. His investigation apparently found that the female deputy had been accompanying the maids when they went into each juror's room to make sure no one was in and the maids could clean.

Tracy's paranoia didn't endear her to anybody, even me, but it was awful watching her torture herself. With her personality traits, she should never have been selected for enforced isolation. She had no way to escape from her inner fears.

Sitting there in the lounge that night at a little table by a picture window, I listened absentmindedly to Tracy prattling on, and looked up to find Jeanette eyeing me. Not angrily. No, tonight it was the smug look, her "I'm gonna git you, sucker" stare that made me nervous. What the hell was wrong with this woman?

It's a question that Lisa and Millie tried to answer for me one day.

"I think Jeanette's whole attitude changed as soon as Tracy Hampton joined our table," said Millie.

"But, why?" I asked. "Tracy's very like-able and never gave anybody any trouble that I could see."

Millie and Lisa shook their heads, the way women do when men just aren't getting it. Said Lisa, "You were the only male at that table when Tracy came. You used to talk to Jeanette a lot, and I think she got jealous of Tracy when you started talking more and more to her."

"Are you saying Jeanette had eyes for me? I absolutely can't believe that."

Lisa and Millie did their head-shaking thing again. "It's not that a woman has to like you," said Millie. "If there's a man around and another woman comes along—and the man starts paying more attention to the new woman—the other woman doesn't like it. She doesn't have to be in love with him. She's just exercising her natural female jealousy."

On February 7, 1995, a sixty-three-year-old white female legal secretary was bounced from the jury. Her removal came in the wake of a run-in she'd had with Jeanette that had turned nasty. It happened out on the patio, where people were walking or jogging for exercise. This old lady was a health nut. She did everything with vigor and energy. She walked fast, she ran fast, and was always on the go. At one point, as she passed Jeanette, she accidentally brushed her. It was just a slight contact but Jeanette went wild. She blew this up into a totally fabricated story that the old white lady had pushed her. It was totally unfair and it disgusted me.

This time I wasn't alone. A couple of black jurors told me that Jeanette's smug, self-righteous attitude was disturbing.

"She sets herself up too high, and she's making a whole lot of trouble out of nothing," snapped one juror.

Said the other: "That was a nice old lady who never bothered anybody."

I've often been asked if Jeanette's claims that white deputies and white jurors were racists are true. Here's the truth: I never saw any deliberate racial attacks by white jurors or deputies against any black jurors. Jeanette's experience was not my experience—and that's the honest-to-God truth. I had no problem with any of the white jurors, including Tracy Kennedy, who was certainly obnoxious but never racist. Tracy Kennedy, as I'll explain, was an equal opportunity pain in the butt. In my experience, the white people who were on that jury bent over backwards to be friendly. I know that some African Americans will be angered by my statement, but that's how I saw it.

I hate racism. It's an attitude I find stupid, no matter who practices it. For one brief period in my own life, I embraced racism, hating white people and blaming them for all my woes. It didn't work for me. It went against my nature, I guess. I'm outgoing. I like people. And one day—just like that—it seemed senseless to dislike one group of fellow human beings solely on the basis of skin color. Racism actually became *tiresome*. I'd get caught up in conversations with people who struck me as interesting or friendly, and then suddenly stop myself and say, hey, this is a white person. You're supposed to hate white people, remember?

I'm not giving a free pass to the entire white race, but just let me repeat what my daddy always told me: "There are bad white people, but there are bad black people, too. Don't judge people by the color of their skin. It's not right when white people do it, and it's not right when black people do it."

Friction built up in our artificial environment. It got totally bizarre at times. Like when Tracy Hampton—who needed a friend probably more than anyone on that jury—snubbed a young woman juror who tried to buddy up with her. This was a white female juror named Lana, who was about Tracy's age. During the time Tracy was whining and fretting to me about nobody liking her, Lana made constant overtures of friendship.

"Tracy, I just don't understand you," I'd say. "Here's Lana wanting to be friends with you and you act all stuck-up. What's the matter with you?"

"I just don't like her," Tracy would pout.

Tracy had made it plain she didn't trust white people, but that wasn't the problem in this case. The problem was Lana's incredible, sexy looks. She was a blonde bombshell. And Tracy just couldn't stand the competition.

"Tracy, why don't you like Lana? She's a terrific young lady. Did you know she's married to a black guy? He's a body-builder. How can you be acting like this when you complain about how Jeanette and the others treat you?"

"Michael, please, I don't want to talk about it."

Minor incidents became major blowups.

One day, Francine wrote a letter to Judge Ito requesting that the deputies who guarded us on the weekends wear civilian clothes rather than uniforms so it wouldn't seem as if we were in a prison-like environment. Most of us had discussed this subject in several conversations and agreed it was a good idea. Francine decided to take action. She wrote a letter to Judge Ito—without informing anyone. When some of the black jurors heard about that, all hell broke loose.

"Who does she think she is, writing a letter to Judge Ito and not telling us about it?" said one.

Chimed another: "No one has the right to send off a letter unless all of us give our permission."

Francine's response? "I don't see what the big problem is. Everybody talked about this and I just thought I'd do something about it. It's what we all wanted, right?"

Judge Ito granted the request. Weekend deputies started showing up in civilian clothes. But even though everyone was happy about it, some folks were still grumbling. It's only my opinion, but I think the fact that Francine is white had a great deal to do with the black jurors' dissatisfaction. And let me repeat, it wasn't ALL the black jurors. Just the usual suspects.

I rarely discussed any of this with Beverly during my nightly calls home. It was too dangerous. Spies and snitches were everywhere. Not to mention the deputies. I'd learned that way back during the jury selection process. In mid-October 1994, when Faye Resnick's book came out, I heard about it and mentioned it to a woman going through the selection process with me. Within *hours*, I was standing in front of Judge Ito, who asked my why I was discussing the book.

I told him, "Judge, I wasn't discussing the book. I don't know anything about the book or what's in it. I simply said to somebody that I heard a book by Faye Resnick had just come out. That's all I said."

Judge Ito let it pass with a warning not to discuss the case.

One night, Beverly asked me, "How about that old black man who didn't like our white baby? Is he still giving you grief?"

I looked around furtively. There was, as

usual, a deputy standing nearby. I sighed and gave Beverly answers that I hoped would be impossible for anyone listening to understand.

"Yeah, it's just the same old thing around here."

"The deputy's standing right there, huh?"

"That's right."

"Has that old man said anything to you?"

"No, not like that."

"You mean he's staring you down?"

"Big time."

Beverly started giggling. "Well, he's over seventy. I don't think he'll try to kick your butt."

I cracked up! The deputy looked over at me, sort of smiling. I could laugh myself sick and he didn't care. As long as I wasn't discussing the case.

Beverly said, "Are you sure you're alright in there? I didn't like all that hostility I've been feeling when I visit."

"Aw, Beverly, don't worry so much. It's a

little warm here, but I'm fine. How's that wild bunch of ours?"

"Reynaldo wants to talk to you, O.K.?"

"Sure, baby. Put that little boy on."

A pause. "Hi, Daddy!"

"Hi, there, son. How're you doing? You being a good boy for your mama?"

"Daddy, I drew a picture today."

"Yeah? What'd you draw . . . a fire engine? You save that and bring it next time you see me . . ."

Thank God for telephones. Without them, we'd all be in straitjackets.

I tried to downplay the tension between Johnson and myself. But the old man had been working himself up into a frenzy ever since he'd seen my wife's baby. His furious glares bored holes in me. When I talked to white jurors, he'd say loudly enough to be heard, "Why is he always talking to them?"

Johnson had a new ally in Fred, the huge juror who looked like what he was—an athlete gone to pot. Fred, we'd all learned, was a bully. Whenever we'd be in the video room and somebody would start to talk, Fred had a habit of suddenly shooting his fist up in the air and glaring at whoever was doing the talking. Johnson and Fred were always looking over at me and muttering. I ignored them. But one day it all came to a head.

It happened at the courthouse. One morning we took a break while the attorneys were having a sidebar in court. Johnson had been glaring at me more intensely than ever that day, ever since breakfast. I don't know exactly what set him off. But as we walked into the ninth floor jury room Johnson was looking back at me and hitting his fist into his hand; making motions like he was going to kick my ass. Fred was there, and was actually trying to calm him down. But Johnson just kept hitting his fist into his hand and glaring at me. I could overhear him saying things like, "That no good son of a bitch!" Again, I tried to ignore him in the jury room. But when we went back into the courtroom, he said to me in a threatening way, "I want to talk to you!"

At the time, I didn't say anything. I was embarrassed more than anything. Everybody was watching and I didn't want the white jurors to witness this black-on-black fighting. And what was I going to do, anyway? Punch out a seventy-year-old man? It was ridiculous.

Later, when we'd gone up to the eleventh floor jury room for lunch, Johnson came over to the table where I was sitting and plunked himself down, still glaring. I shook my head and got up. I moved to another table. But Johnson persisted. He approached me later and hissed: "I want to talk to you. And I'm gonna . . ." He didn't finish his threat. He just glared. "Damn this old man," I thought. "I've had enough."

I said, "O.K., Johnson, let's go into the men's room and straighten this out."

He followed me to the men's room. There was a marshal in there, so we just acted like we were in there for business. After the marshal left, I said: "O.K., let's have it out! What is your problem with me?"

The old man was so angry and agitated his jaws were shaking. He kept pointing at me, shaking his finger in my face. I thought, This guy's in great shape for his age and he's acting like he actually might take a swing at me.

"I thought you were different, Michael," Johnson snarled.

"What the hell does that mean?"

"Don't you play games with me," he said. "You know what I'm talking about. Why are you always kissing up to those white people?"

Johnson ranted on and on. For a moment, I was itching to grab that old trouble-maker and slam him up against the wall. There's nothing that makes a black man angrier than being accused of "tomming"—acting like an Uncle Tom. In Johnson's book, that's what I was, only because I had conversations with white jurors. This was pure racial hatred and it made me furious!

"I'll talk to anybody I damn well please," I shouted back at him. "Don't go laying your bad trip on me, old man. I treat people the way they treat me, and I don't care what color they are."

Rage shook the old man. He looked like he was ready to get busy on me.

"You shouldn't be talking to those white people. You stick to your own kind."

Angry as I was at him for yelling in my

202

face, and for hating my white baby, I knew Mr. Johnson had experienced the wide-open racism that used to lead to lynchings in the Deep South. He'd seen the flaming crosses of the Ku Klux Klan back in times so bad that a black man could be randomly stopped on the streets and whipped by white supremacists, who feared no retaliation from the law.

Suddenly, I felt weary, depleted.

This confrontation was pathetic. I had to end it. I said to Johnson: "We can stand here yelling at each other and all, but you know I'm not going to give in and neither are you, so what's the answer? How do we work this out?"

The old man stopped ranting. He calmed down, then he sighed and shook his head.

"There's only one way to do this, Michael. I won't talk to you again and you won't talk to me."

"That's fine with me."

"Fine."

20

⚖️

Trial Chronology

FEBRUARY 8–FEBRUARY 12, 1995

Wednesday
February 8, 1995

29th day of sequestration
Jury present

- Eva Stein, a neighbor of Nicole Simpson on Bundy, testified that she was awakened by loud barking at 10:15 P.M.

- Louis Karpf, Eva Stein's fiancé, testified he was outside getting his mail at 11:00 P.M. when he was frightened by Kato the dog.

- Steven Schwab testified he was walking his dog in the neighborhood when he saw an Akita with bloody paws. He took the dog to his apartment.

- Sukru Boztepe, Schwab's neighbor, testified that he and his wife walked their dog and it led them to discover Nicole's body.

- Elsie Tistaert, an elderly woman who lived nearby, testified that she heard a dog barking for about thirty minutes at around the same time.

Jury not present

- Judge Ito declined to quash the subpoena for Marguerite Simpson Thomas, first wife of O.J. Simpson. Mrs. Thomas claimed through her attorney, Carl Jones, that the document was served illegally.

- Defense witness Mary Anne Gerchas was booked in West Los Angeles on felony grand theft and fraud charges.

• Judge Ito determined that it was inappropriate for Marcia Clark to wear her angel pin.

Thursday
February 9, 1995

30th day of sequestration
Jury present

• Pictures of the crime scene were revealed in court as LAPD officer Robert Riske, first officer on the scene, described what he saw. Mr. and Mrs. Brown, parents of slain Nicole Brown Simpson, exited the courtroom before the photos were shown. Mrs. Goldman and Kim Goldman remained in court, with Kim crying quietly. Marcia Clark conducted the questioning of Robert Riske, the only witness of the day.

• Judge Ito told the jurors that they would be going on a field trip to Brentwood.

Jury not present

• Prosecutor William Hodgman returned to work today. He will function as prosecution team manager outside the courtroom.

Friday
February 10, 1995

31st day of sequestration
Court not in session

• Today Judge Lance Ito led lawyers from both sides on a preview tour of the Brentwood area. The official jury tour is scheduled to take place on Sunday.

Saturday
February 11, 1995

32nd day of sequestration

Sunday
February 12, 1995

33rd day of sequestration

• The jury field trip took place today.

21

⚖️

The Field Trip

FEBRUARY 12, 1995

News that we were going on a field trip to Nicole Brown Simpson's condominium and O.J. Simpson's estate in Brentwood had hit us as a total surprise. The night before, Saturday night, the deputies got us all assembled and talked about the field trip. It's hard to describe the excitement. Finally, we were going to visit the scene of the crime. Now when the attorneys used terms like "the condo entryway," or "the area behind Kato's apartment," we'd all focus on the same sharp picture in our minds. Now we'd actually follow the "trail of blood" that the prosecution had described in opening statements as stretching from Nicole's condo on Bundy to

O.J.'s house on Rockingham. We wouldn't actually see the blood, of course. It had long since been cleaned up. I make mention of this because one of the jurors actually asked nervously if there would be blood at the scene.

One of the deputies started running down the ground rules. He told us, "There will be very strict rules about not talking to anyone else when you get to the crime scene. Here are a few things to remember . . ."

Oh, boy. More rules to memorize. But nobody was moaning and groaning. Visiting the crime scene was exciting all by itself, but somehow the idea that we'd actually drive across the familiar streets of our city and see other human beings going about their daily lives seemed almost magical. We weren't looking at this field trip like it was a day at the beach. But day-in, day-out enforced isolation made us hunger for fresh sights and sounds.

We woke up early that Sunday morning. We were lined up, marched down to the underground parking garage beneath the hotel, and loaded into our vans. Then we were whisked across town to the courthouse on Temple Street. We waited in the underground parking lot for awhile. Everybody kept asking, "What's the delay? Why are we sitting here?"

Because we'd been cut off from the outside world, and had no access to newspapers, radio, or TV reports about the O.J. case, we didn't know about the circus-like atmosphere that had blown up out of control since the trial had actually started. It's not that we didn't know the O.J. Simpson case was a major event. But we'd been shut away from the world for more than a month and we weren't aware that America was now in a total O.J. frenzy. And we didn't know, sitting there in that parking garage, that we were about to become the focal point of the most elaborate security operation for a motorcade ever mounted by Los Angeles law enforcement authorities. Judge Ito had demanded extraordinary precautions for the jurors' protection. And he got it.

Suddenly, the order to "Move out!"

crackled over the deputies' radios. The vans accelerated. We shot out of the underground parking lot and exited on Temple Street, and couldn't believe our eyes. An army of policemen and sheriff's deputies and marshals surrounded us. Helicopters whirred overhead. I counted twenty-five police cars—then stopped counting. There were more than two dozen policemen on motorcycles and, off in the distance, an army of media vehicles.

"Wow . . ." "Oh, my God . . ." "What the hell . . ." "I've never seen so many cops . . ."

It was unbelievable. The escort to end all escorts. As we roared across Los Angeles towards Brentwood, we saw that streets were cordoned off so no one could cut across our path. Someone thought they'd seen police snipers on buildings along the route as we left the downtown area, but I have no idea if that's true. This looked heavier than any presidential motorcade I've ever seen. When we hit the outskirts of the upscale Brentwood area, it was like driving through a carnival. The jury motorcade was still many blocks from Nicole's address on Bundy when the crowd started getting big. People were lining the streets, cheering like we were on parade. Car horns were honking. It reminded me of The Chase, when people parked their vehicles on the side of the road and got out to cheer for O.J.

Our vans pulled up to the Bundy address. There we got another rundown of the rules. Each of us would be given tags that marked us as jurors. We were told that we would be taken into the house in groups of four or five. We were instructed to view the crime scene carefully and, above all, not to say anything to anyone. Total silence was the rule. It was going to take some time. Each group would take up to thirty minutes to view the crime scene and the interior of the condo, and there were four or five groups.

Like everyone else, I was peering out the van windows at America's most notorious murder site. The entryway beyond the gate near the street literally overflowed with trees and shrubs. I remember hearing people ask, on TV and radio shows, why no one had heard the murders take place. After seeing the entryway close up, my opinion is that any cries by the victims would have been largely muffled by that mini-jungle of shrubbery. A perfect place to commit a murder—especially in the dark, I thought. It was a very nice condo. Not new, but nice. I shook my head as I looked around at this community of wealth and privilege. I thought, Uptown or downtown, murder is murder. Rich folks get just as crazy as poor folks, and for the same old reasons.

Finally, it was my turn to tour the site. I joined my group, which included Millie, Tracy, and Lisa. We assembled on the sidewalk, waiting for the deputies to lead us in. Off in the distance, being held back by police, were hordes of reporters, photographers, and TV cameramen. From my impressions as we'd motored into Brentwood, there were possibly 150 members of the press corps in the area.

Finally, the deputies opened the gate and I stepped into the entryway to Nicole's condo. It was a chilling experience. I'll never forget it. For a moment, I imagined I could feel the essence of those two people I'd never met, but had come to know so well. Now I was standing on the very spot where they had struggled for their lives and lost. Little shivers ran over my skin.

As I looked straight ahead at where they'd fallen, those gory crime scene photos we were shown on that first day of the trial flashed into my mind. There, at the bottom of the steps lay Nicole, her blood flowing down to the spot where I now stood. Over there to my right, Ron Goldman lay dead, frozen in the very act of fighting back. Nicole looked almost peaceful. Ron's body exuded agony.

I blinked my eyes and the pictures went away. Now I was looking at the crime scene cleaned up and neutral. And what struck me most was a fact that became so frighteningly obvious when you saw it in real life: Ron Goldman had died in a trap. He was backed up against the high metal gate located at the rear of the entryway and just to the right of the steps. When you actually stand in the entryway, it's much narrower than you realize from photos or TV. Back where Ron had been trapped, it was a perfect little cul-de-sac, a dead end. If he'd been fighting a man of any size at all, there'd be no escape. Ron was boxed in. The gate at his back, trees and shrubbery to the left and right of him. No way to escape but straight ahead, straight into the flailing arms of the knife-wielding maniac who'd killed him. No way out. None.

Now we walked into the condo. As I entered the house, I saw Chris Darden and Johnnie Cochran standing together like old pals. It surprised me. In the courtroom, they act like they hate each other. Johnnie Cochran looked at me and something registered in his eyes. I don't know what it was. But it was more than the casual look you give to someone you've seen many times before. Then he looked away.

I looked at Chris Darden and I recoiled. I later told my wife that Darden gave me "a look of death." I know that sounds overly dramatic, but I'll never forget that evil eye. I learned later that what must have prompted his glowering stare were my clothes. The night before, when we'd been told about the field trip, the deputies had warned us that the forecast showed a possibility for rain. That morning, I'd decided to wear my favorite cap and jacket—and both were marked with the emblem of the San Francisco Forty-Niners football team.

That fact was widely reported in the press, I learned later. And it was probably why Chris Darden and Marcia Clark had launched a full-scale investigation into my background. They interpreted the Forty-Niners jacket and cap as a sign that I was "pro O.J." I've always found that conclusion a little bit stupid. Millions of American men wear jackets and caps that sport their team emblem, and the San Francisco Forty-Niners had won the Super Bowl just weeks before.

But the prosecutors should have considered two other facts before they decided I was another O.J. fan:

1. Although O.J. had played for the Forty-Niners at the end of his career, his true fame comes from his early career with the Buffalo Bills.

2. My brother works for the Forty-Niners as a public relations man. That's why I was wearing that cap and jacket. And, ironically, I wouldn't have been wearing them at all if the weatherman hadn't made the wrong forecast for Sunday.

Now it was time to visit O.J. Simpson's estate. Our motorcade—and what I figured was about two hundred cops—motored over to Rockingham. The deputies parked the vans and we had to stay inside while all the logistics were figured out. Eventually, Marcia Clark, Christopher Darden, Johnnie Cochran, all the other lawyers, a court reporter, Judge Ito, and O.J. Simpson were standing outside talking. It looked like they were making some last-minute deals.

Then Judge Ito came walking over to our van, just as the deputies told us to file on out. The judge came pushing his way into the van, actually bucking the line. That's when he told us not to look at any of the photographs in O.J.'s house. I heard what he said, but all I could think of was getting out of that van and into the sunshine.

O.J.'s estate wasn't a land-poor location like the Bundy condo. Here you could really stretch your legs. I think all of us had lightened up a little bit at this point knowing that the worst of it—the murder scene—was behind us. We all relaxed a bit and walked around outside. And maybe that's how I lost my concentration and forgot what Judge Ito had said. At any rate, by the time I got into O.J.'s house, I reacted with great curiosity to the hundreds of photographs hung in frames throughout the house. I started looking at them intently.

Suddenly, I sensed that my friend Millie was giving me a pointed glare, arching her eyebrows like "Didn't you hear what the judge said?" It hit me then what I was doing. I backed away from the photos. By then, I guess, it was too late.

The jurors were taken all through O.J.'s house. Then we went out to the backyard area next to the swimming pool. This was the spot where O.J. supposedly chipped golf shots on the night of the murders. Then we walked down to the infamous guesthouse occupied by Kato Kaelin. We actually saw where the bloody glove was found by Mark Fuhrman. We inspected the back wall where Kato said he had heard three thumps. We checked the air conditioning unit, the back fence . . . everything. But what made it eerie was that nobody uttered a word. Nobody. Not the marshals, not the jurors. The only sounds were birds chirping.

Later, before we got back into the vans, I stopped for a long look at O.J.'s house. It was nice, but I've seen nicer places. It was an older house, not glamorous at all. One thing struck me: The place had the feel of an elaborate bachelor pad, not the home of a family man.

On the trip back to our hotel, we were pretty quiet. I sensed that we were all sifting through the memories of what we'd just seen, putting facts we'd heard into a fresh perspective now that we'd viewed the actual sites involved in the double murder. Events we'd only heard about seemed much more sharply focused now. And in a strange way, I felt a real connection with the victims, Ron and Nicole. Somebody had committed this vicious, tragic crime. Someone had to pay.

A few days later, the jurors got to take another trip—this time to a Target store. It was a terrific day, despite the fact that it was drizzling, and we all had a great time. Especially Jeanette Harris. That's why I was astounded when Jeanette announced to the world, the press, and Judge Ito that racism had reared its ugly head on a Target trip. Jeanette's story was that white deputies allowed white jurors to shop longer than black jurors. Yet I clearly remember that after we got back to the hotel from Target, Jeanette was standing around with the rest of us talking about what a great time she'd had.

It was just before Valentine's Day. We all had shopping to do for the holiday and were excited at the idea of getting out again. As I recall, there were five white deputies escorting us that day. I particularly remember that the deputy in charge was a very nice guy. We were ushered through the Target store in groups—the same groups we'd been in for the field trip to Bundy and Rockingham. The only rule was, we had to stay away from the counters where we might see tabloids or magazines with O.J. stories. But that was it. We weren't pushed or pressed to hurry up. We all got our shopping done and had a great time, laughing and talking and buying Valentine's Day surprises for our next Family Day.

As a matter of fact, when my group left the store, we found Jeanette Harris and her group already outside. They had paid for their items and were ready to board the vans and leave. If her group of black jurors had been hustled outside by the white deputies, why hadn't the same thing happened to my group of black jurors? The answer is, nothing of the sort occurred.

Once again, I disagree with Jeanette Harris. And it's important to say that after six weeks of sequestration, I *never* saw any hint of racism directed at black jurors by white deputies. It never happened to me, I never saw it happen to anyone else, and not one juror ever told me of racism directed at them. To be fair, perhaps Jeanette Harris was talking about some other trip to Target. After all, she spent more time on the jury than I did.

Ask yourself this question: After Judge Ito removed three white sheriff's deputies from juror guard duty—apparently because of Jeanette's racism charges—why did the majority of the jurors come to court wearing black? It was a revolt against Judge Ito's decision—but even more, against the mean-spirited attack on the white deputies and jurors by Jeanette Harris!

22 | ⚖️
Trial Chronology

FEBRUARY 23–FEBRUARY 28, 1995

Thursday
February 23, 1995

45th day of sequestration
Jury present

• Cross-examination by Johnnie Cochran of Detective Tom Lange.

• Judge Ito interrupted cross-examination to call a sidebar after the interrogation by Cochran and the replies by Lange were contentious. There were numerous objections from the prosecution about the hostility.

Judge Ito hastily ordered the jury out as the sidebar turned into a brouhaha. There was a stand-off between Judge Ito and Christopher Darden, who refused to apologize for sidebar remarks that he'd made about Johnnie Cochran's derogatory statements. Ito cited Darden for contempt, but then vacated the citation. Finally, Darden apologized and Judge Ito apologized to him.

- The jury was excused until Monday, as Rosa Lopez is scheduled to appear tomorrow.

Friday
February 24, 1995

46th day of sequestration
Jury not present

- Prospective defense witness Rosa Lopez was in court. She is expected to testify for O.J. Simpson, saying that she saw his Bronco parked in the street outside his house at the time of the murders.

- The defense requested that Rosa Lopez be permitted to testify on videotape in case she should flee the country.

- Under questioning by Christopher Darden, Lopez was caught in several outright lies.

- The defense was agreeable to videotaping her testimony at 6:00 P.M., after an already extended day in court. Judge Ito wanted the jury to hear her testimony live, so he ordered the jury brought to court for the 6:00 P.M. testimony.

Jury present

- Jurors were hastily brought to court in their leisure attire, only to be told by Judge Ito that it was a false alarm. He apologized for the inconvenience and they were returned to their sequestered housing.

Saturday
February 25, 1995

47th day of sequestration

Sunday
February, 26, 1995

48th day of sequestration

Monday
February 27, 1995

49th day of sequestration
Jury not present

• Defense witness Rosa Lopez's testimony was videotaped for use later during the defense case.

• Prosecutor Marcia Clark asked Judge Ito for sanctions against the defense for again failing to provide discovery, this time regarding a document containing an interview with Rosa Lopez.

• Defense private investigator Bill Pavelic testified that an audiotape had also been made during that Lopez interview, even though defense attorney Carl Douglas had stated that there was no tape.

• Judge Ito said that he will not impose sanctions until the tape of Rosa Lopez becomes part of the defense case. There was considerable speculation that the testimony of Rosa Lopez will not be played.

Tuesday
February 28, 1995

50th day of sequestration
Jury not present

• Part of today's session was held in chambers where the lawyers and Judge Ito played the Rosa Lopez tape.

• Judge Ito ordered the defense to pay for Rosa Lopez's hotel accommodations while she is waiting to resume testimony.

• This afternoon Rosa Lopez told Judge Ito that she was tired and didn't want any more questions. He ordered her to return to court on Thursday.

23 | ⚖⚖
Fights

Rosa Lopez really shook up the O.J. jury. Judge Ito didn't want her testimony heard by us, so for several days starting on February 23, we were kept out of the courtroom. You remember how your mama used to tell you that the devil loves idle hands. Well, there were lots of idle hands in the jury that week, and that's when the devil really started raising hell.

The same old cliques and rivalries I've described were still causing tension. The new thorn in everybody's side was Tracy Kennedy, or "T.K.," as he likes to be called. It was almost refreshing that, for once, blacks and whites agreed on one thing: T.K. was an arrogant, obnoxious boor. For the black jurors, just looking at T.K. was like waving a red flag in a bull's face because he's the spitting image of Colonel Sanders—snow-white hair, white moustache and pointed chin. T.K. liked to tell people he was part American Indian, but he looked like some actor Central Casting would send over if you asked for a typical, pre–Civil War white plantation overseer.

T.K. lacked sensitivity whenever he was around black people. He'd sit down next to you on a sofa, spread his legs and sprawl all over, then put his feet up on the coffee table. What's wrong with that, you ask? African Americans are probably a bit oversensitive on this point, but after many years of having to swallow racial insults in silence, we're suspicious of white people's attitudes. So when a white man who looks like Colonel Sanders approaches a group of black people, they're checking him out to see if he respects them. And sprawling all over like you own the place isn't a good way to connect with strangers, black OR white.

The reaction of white jurors to T.K. was

much less complicated. They simply marked him as a total jerk and avoided him whenever possible.

T.K. had some really bad habits. First of all, he loved picking out a sofa that he'd sprawl over so that he could keep it all to himself. And he drove people nuts with a stunt he used to pull in the telephone room. He'd sit down in a chair near the windowsill, remove his shoes and socks and put his naked feet up on the windowsill. It was a disgusting sight. More than one juror had occasion to cut a telephone call short when Tracy indulged in this crude behavior. His feet stank!

Frankly, I don't think T.K. gave a damn whether he annoyed people or not; or if he was even aware that he did. He was very much a man into his own thoughts and concerns. T.K. gave the impression that he always had a big deal up his sleeve. On the day when we all learned we'd been selected for the O.J. jury, and were starting to get acquainted, the first thing T.K. ever said to me was: "I have to get my computer in here. I just have to get my computer in here."

He had a strange way of repeating phrases like that, almost as if he were giving himself a pep talk, reminding himself that he had to deliver the goods.

I said, "Why do you need your computer, T.K.?"

He gave me a sort of sly, superior look, raising his eyebrows and winking, as if he were letting me in on some big secret. "Well, it's all about business, isn't it? It's all about business!"

"I understand what you're talking about—I understand where you're coming from," I said. Then I thought, Damn! Now he's got me talking like him, repeating everything.

Strangely enough, I really did understand where T.K. was coming from. There's no doubt in my mind that he was talking about writing a book about his experiences on the O.J. jury. And later, of course, he was removed from the jury when it was reported that deputies had found computer disks in his room with notes about the case.

I never heard anyone on the jury say out loud, "Someday I'm going to write a book about this." But I know it crossed everybody's mind. How could it not? And there were always remarks like, "People wouldn't believe what goes on around here . . ." Or, "This has got to be the biggest murder trial of all time." I know the thought went through my mind, but it was an idle thought. With T.K., you sensed that if anyone wrote a book, he'd be the one.

Even the deputies bristled at T.K.'s brusque, arrogant ways. I remember one day when he decided he wanted to go outside for exercise. He approached a Deputy Scott—a young fellow about twenty-six years old—and told him he wanted to go out to the patio. Deputy Scott said, "O.K., but I'll have to go out first and make sure the area is secure." That was routine and normal. Jurors never went outside until deputies checked to make sure no one was in the area. It was for our safety. There is always some nut looking to make a name for himself.

But T.K. got right in Deputy Scott's face and said, "I don't need to wait around for you to do anything. I'm going outside." Then T.K. stood right in Deputy Scott's path and eyeballed him for a long moment. It got really tense. I thought the deputy was going to shove T.K., who stood there as if blocking his path. It was bizarre behavior, even for T.K. I remember thinking that he might be feeling the pressure of everyone either avoiding him or ostracizing him outright. Finally, T.K. backed off and sat down. Deputy Scott went outside, did his job, then came back in and told T.K. he could go out.

A couple of days later, T.K. had a run-in with a Deputy Russell, who was black. I got there just as it was ending and didn't hear exactly what was said. But it was a really heated conversation. T.K. was right in Deputy Russell's face, literally giving him hell. After it broke up, I asked one of the white female jurors what had happened.

"Tracy almost got his ass kicked, that's what happened," she said. "And he was asking for it. That man is disgusting. He's a disgrace to the white race."

That's exactly what she said and I'll never forget how furious she was. My sense of it was that she thought T.K. was indulging in racist behavior, because Deputy Russell is black. It's possible T.K. has a problem with black authority figures. But I don't think that was it because he'd just had a similar run-in with a white deputy. The fight with Deputy Russell apparently started over the same thing he'd been fighting about with Deputy Scott. T.K. had wanted to go outside to jog and didn't like having to ask permission. People who'd witnessed the tense encounter told me they had really feared that T.K. and Deputy Russell were going to come to blows.

Incidents like this escalated the tension. Every juror, black and white, wanted to avoid T.K. But that's a problem when you're sequestered. You can't avoid anyone. There's no escape, nowhere to get away to for a few hours and just blow off steam. People get on your nerves. Tempers flare. And finally somebody snaps.

A couple of days after the T.K. incident, we were transported from the courthouse back to the hotel. We got out of the vans in the parking garage and headed over to a freight elevator. Several people got in and were standing there waiting for the doors to close. I'd been lagging a bit and I walked faster so I'd be in the elevator before the doors started to close. Fred, the huge juror who liked to bully people, was inside the elevator standing at the front of the group.

As I approached, he moved as if to intercept me and said, "There's no more room. Catch the next elevator." I stopped, genuinely puzzled. It was a big elevator and there was plenty of room.

"What are you talking about, Fred?"

He repeated, "There isn't any room. You can't get in."

I walked into the elevator, pushing Fred aside. He grabbed my arm and started to tug at me. I gave him a good shove and said something like, "You don't want to mess with me, Fred! I'm in shape and you're not!"

Lisa and Millie were in the elevator and they immediately started chewing Fred out, saying, "What's wrong with you? There's plenty of room. Who put you in charge of things? You're lucky we let YOU in the elevator."

Now Fred looked embarrassed. He kept his mouth shut for the rest of that day. The rest of us laughed and talked about it, but somebody mentioned that Fred's bullying was getting to be a serious problem. There was talk of sending a letter to Judge Ito. Nothing happened at that point, but I think the news of Fred getting physical with me started percolating, sort of made people think. Then, a couple of days later, Fred almost got into another brawl, this time with Carl.

It was in the video room. People were sitting around watching a movie, and Carl started commenting about a scene. As he'd done so many times before, Fred turned around, flung his clenched fist over his head and glared at Carl. That was Fred's gentle way of telling you, "Shut up!"

It wasn't the first time Fred and Carl had tangled over Fred's bullying. This time it got ugly. For a moment, it looked like they were going to trade punches. Then Carl backed down. I think he was intimidated by Fred's size, and who could blame him. Fred intimidated everyone, including me, despite my brave talk in the elevator. Later, all the jurors were buzzing with this latest incident. Somebody, referring to Carl's mega-bad breath, cracked: "Carl should have breathed on him."

"Yeah, it would have killed him!"

The next day the jurors had an impromptu meeting about Fred's bullying. It was on the morning of March 1, in the ninth floor jury room, shortly before Judge Ito called me into his chambers. A verbal free-for-all had started as we waited to be called into court. People were getting fed up with each other's idiosyncrasies and were starting to talk about it. What really had people pissed off were Fred's threatening gestures every time somebody opened their mouth in the video room. Francine told Fred, "Look, we are all adults here. Who are you to tell us we can't talk in the video room or make comments?"

Fred replied, "Well, I have no problem with you talking. But extra gibberish disturbs me."

Now everybody started criticizing Fred. And at some point, Francine sent word to Judge Ito that she wanted to be released from the jury. I remember Jeanette Harris sat right next to Fred as he took all this heat. As usual, Jeanette didn't open her mouth. But her eyes told you where she stood.

Man, this is getting bad, I thought. What's going to happen here?

My answer was just moments away.

24 ⚖️
The Jury Room

MARCH 1, 1995

10:15 A.M.

"Juror Number 620!"

Deirdre Robertson was standing in the doorway of the ninth floor jury room. It probably wasn't more than ten minutes since Judge Ito had dismissed me from his chambers to sweat out his decision on whether I'd remain an O.J. juror.

It had been a long ten minutes. Nobody had spoken to me. That had angered me at first, until I came to the slow realization that I really had nothing to say either. Everyone knew that you weren't called into Judge Ito's chambers unless something serious had happened. It was up to me to reveal my troubles, if I chose. Nobody wanted the distasteful task of prying it out of me.

Moments later, I was walking with Deirdre towards Judge Ito's chambers for the second time that morning. Once again, Deirdre knocked on the door, opened it, and stood aside. I walked in and faced the same cast of characters, all those famous faces: Judge Ito, Marcia Clark, Robert Shapiro, Johnnie Cochran, Chris Darden. I sat down and read my fate in Judge Ito's unsmiling eyes even before he spoke. The meeting was brutally brief. In less than a minute, I was walking back out of Judge Ito's chambers.

I was no longer an O.J. juror!

It had happened so fast, it's still a blur. Judge Ito said something like, "Mr. Knox, the fact that you failed to reveal on your jury questionnaire that you had once been charged with kidnapping is something I cannot ignore. I have decided to relieve you of your jury duty. If you had revealed the charge at the proper time, perhaps we could have worked with you. But now I have no choice.

"I'm instructing you not to talk about

your experiences on the jury for ninety days and you must not reveal the location of the hotel where the jurors are sequestered . . ." And I think he promised that he wouldn't tell the press about the kidnapping charge.

That's all I remember. The next moment, Deirdre Robertson was leading me over to a bench out in the hallway. She said kindly, "Mr. Knox, why don't you just sit here for a few minutes?" She left me alone. A few minutes later, I looked up to see Deputy Russell standing over me. He smiled and said, "Well, that's the way it goes sometimes."

I nodded. Then I said, "Deputy Russell, can I ask you to do a favor for me? I'd rather not go back into the jury room and I was . . ."

He held up his hand, cutting me off. "Don't worry about it. There's no need for you to go back in there. I'll get your things and bring them out to you."

Deputy Russell walked off toward the ninth floor jury room. I sat there, numb. Random emotions flashed through me as my mind tried to figure out whether I was happy or sad. I was barely aware of people passing by in the hallway. Then I saw Deirdre heading toward the jury room. I'll bet she's going to tell one of the alternates that they're replacing me on the jury, I thought. I smiled at Deirdre as she walked past, half hoping she'd stop and tell me who it would be. But she just nodded and kept walking. My guess was that Francine would replace me. I knew Judge Ito liked her sense of humor. What a surprise when it turned out I was right.

Deputy Russell came back carrying the briefcase I always carted around. He grinned. "Well, you're going to get out of here early today," he said jovially. I stood and followed him to the elevators. Moments later, we were in a sheriff's car, accelerating up out of the basement parking garage and into the Los Angeles sunshine.

I was a free man. Back at the hotel, Deputy Russell and a deputy named Higgins came along to my room and helped me pack. Deputy Russell snapped his fingers at one point, as if he'd forgotten something, and said, "Deputy Higgins, would you go and get those dry cleaning bills and telephone bills for Mr. Knox?"

I fell for it hook, line, and sinker. "What

cleaning bills and telephone bills? Why should I be paying those?"

Deputy Russell shook his head regretfully. "I'm sorry, Mr. Knox, but you are no longer a ward of the state. You have to pay your own bills now, isn't that right, Deputy Higgins?"

"That's absolutely right, Deputy Russell. I wonder why nobody explained that to Mr. Knox?"

By now, of course, I got the gag. I laughed and said, "Why are you guys trying to drive me crazy? I'm under a big mental strain here."

It was one of those moments you don't forget easily. Here were two men I didn't really know, and would probably never see again, kidding around, and trying to make me feel better. I was touched. And it worked. Then Deputy Russell drove me home to Long Beach.

In light of the firestorm Jeanette Harris unleashed when she accused white deputies of anti-black racism, I want to say this again loud and clear: Every deputy who guarded the jury treated us with professionalism and respect. And I never heard any juror, *including Jeanette*, complain about white-on-black racism by the deputies. That's the God-honest truth.

As I rolled down the freeway with Deputy Russell at the wheel, I looked forward to a big homecoming. I just concentrated on the joy of seeing Beverly and the kids and my dog. I wanted to crack a beer, kick back and catch up on what everybody had been doing. And most of all, I wanted to turn on the TV set, watch the evening news—and hear all about O.J.

Does that sound crazy? Probably. But for nearly two months the jurors and I, even though we had ringside seats at the Trial of the Century, knew that more was happening outside the court than we ever heard about. Every time Judge Ito told us to leave the courtroom, we knew we were missing out on something juicy. Enquiring minds want to know, so I could hardly wait to watch TV, listen to the radio, and read newspapers that didn't have big holes where O.J. stories had been cut out by deputies.

Curiosity. It's the high-octane additive

that separates man from beast. We human beings love to know the news. That's why I shouldn't have been surprised when I pulled up to the house and saw a white TV truck and about ten reporters milling around.

Beverly and the kids came out to greet me and Deputy Russell helped fend off the reporters, who were firing questions at me, until we all got back into the house. After a round of kisses and hugs, I grabbed that beer I'd been looking forward to, then sat down and asked Beverly what was going on, what she'd heard.

Beverly rolled her eyes. "You mean, what haven't I heard," she said. "These reporters are saying all kinds of crazy things. Did you make some kind of bet about whether O.J. was guilty or innocent with somebody at work?"

"Oh, wow!" I said, shaking my head in disbelief. "How the hell have these guys heard about that stupid rumor? Did somebody from the court announce that?"

"I don't think so," said Beverly. "I didn't hear it on the news. But since these reporters started showing up, I haven't had much time to keep up with what's going on. But I'll tell you one thing—my mother called from Louisiana, wanting to know why I didn't leave you if you're a wife beater."

I stared back at Beverly in total shock. "What? Wife beating? What the hell are you talking about?"

Beverly was giggling. "She said she heard it on the news. I had to swear to my mother that you weren't beating me. I told her it was probably just some rumors the reporters had started. This is getting absolutely crazy."

Somebody was knocking on the door. The phone started ringing. I automatically went over to pick it up and Beverly said, "Don't answer that unless you want to talk to Ted Koppel or Katie Couric. Or Maury Povich." She started giggling again.

"What are you talking about, baby?"

"They've all called, Michael. They all want to talk to you. I feel so privileged to be married to a big star."

Somebody was really pounding on the door now. I ignored the phone and walked over to the window. I couldn't believe what I saw. Now there were at least twenty-five reporters outside. The phone kept ringing. It would stop for a few seconds and start ringing again. Damn.

I swear, at that moment all I wanted to do was watch TV. I just wanted to sit down in my favorite chair, finish my first homecoming beer, and hear some news. But . . .

Curiosity. It got the better of me. I picked up the phone.

"Michael Knox? Hi, I'm a producer for Ted Koppel of 'Nightline'. I guess you've heard that Ted is very anxious to speak to you and if you'll just hold for a moment, I'll put him right on for you . . ."

Before that day ended, I had spoken directly to Ted Koppel, Katie Couric, Connie Chung, and producers for God knows how many other famous TV and radio shows. Katie Couric insisted on giving me her home phone number. And when I finally walked outside my house, there must have been about thirty-five reporters and TV cameramen. It was unbelievable. They were all trying to talk to me, to get an interview. I finally said a few words on what it was like being a juror, and that I was amazed to hear some of the bizarre rumors they'd asked me about. I denied I was a wife beater. Then I got worried about saying too much and went back into the house.

I'd never handled anything like this before. The press was unbelievably aggressive. The crowd just kept swelling until there were about fifty reporters outside. There was even a helicopter flying over my house. A helicopter!

Beverly got a little panicky and called some friends to come over and help us. We actually started worrying that the reporters and cameramen were going to push through our front door and take over the house. It got so bad that my son's karate instructor, a black belt, finally stationed himself outside the front door and backed them off.

I wasn't angry with the press. But they were incredibly pushy. I just couldn't believe that everybody wanted to talk to me. The other thing that struck me was how they'd throw a sensational question at you, then get sort of bored when you told them their information was wrong and you attempted to explain in depth. These guys wanted "yes" or "no" answers.

"Do you deny charges of spousal abuse?"

"Did you make a bet that O.J. Simpson would walk away from the trial a free man?"

I denied both reports. But they just continued to hammer at me. What really infuriated me later was that one of the major TV networks had interviewed a couple of my co-workers at Federal Express and asked them if the allegations that I'd made a bet about O.J. were true. My co-workers, a man and a woman, told the network reporter that it was totally false. That network, which had originally broadcast the allegation, never cleared things up by airing the follow-up interview with my co-workers saying that I'd never made any O.J. bets.

What a homecoming day! It was almost frightening. Finally, my brother, who works for the San Francisco Forty-Niners, was on the phone and I got some expert advice.

"Michael, you've said enough. Don't say anything more to the reporters. Just ignore them totally and they'll finally get the message and leave. It's a mistake to say anything right now. You're tired and I suggest you get a good night's sleep."

I put the phone down and walked outside to face the mob of reporters. They all started yelling questions. I held up my arms until they finally quieted down. Then I said, "I can't say anything more to you. I won't be making any more statements. I'm going to bed, ladies and gentlemen, it's all over."

But it wasn't.

25 ⚖ Aftermath

MAY 30, 1995

That's my story. The O.J. jury, up close and personal with Michael Knox. It's the way I saw it, as honestly as I can recall it. Telling my story is the scariest thing I've ever done. I'm just an average guy, working two jobs, trying to feed my family and have a decent life. I've never seen my thoughts put down on paper. How many people have? In junior high school they told us, "The pen is mightier than the sword." Now I understand exactly what that means. Words, written down, kick ass!

My story's going to infuriate some people. Every "O.J. Book"—from Faye Resnick's, to O.J.'s, to Kato's—has pissed off one side or the other. There's tremendous passion in the O.J. case and that's why it has polarized America. Anyone who gets involved becomes an instant newsmaker. Who could have predicted that someday Ted Koppel or Katie Couric would—even briefly—be hanging on Michael Knox's every word?

Well, news media, you asked for it! You came banging on my door, insisting I should tell all. What you really meant, I now realize, was that I should tell YOU all. So that YOU could get the scoop, the bucks, and the glory. But I decided I didn't want my story reduced to a couple of quick TV sound bites. Or four quotes in the daily paper. I had something to say, and I'm saying it. My way . . . with a little help from my friends. I know it's going to drive you media guys nuts because you've got the lock on buying and selling people's stories. And I know that most of you reporters are going to get right in my face and say: "Knox, you wrote this book for the money, didn't you? Don't you think it's wrong to profit off this terrible tragedy?"

Here's my honest answer to Question One: "No—and Yes!"

And my honest answer to Question Two: "Don't be such jive hypocrites, Mr. and Ms. Media! You guys profit off tragedy every day. This is my story and I've got every right to tell it MY way. I'm just trying to set the record straight after you guys got it wrong. You labeled me a wife beater and a guy who's irresponsible enough to gamble a week's hard-earned salary on some stupid bet about O.J. Simpson."

Tragedy? I'll give you tragedy! Here's an exclusive story that was picked up in major newspapers:

National Enquirer, May 23, 1995—Just one day after she convinced Judge Lance Ito to let her off the O.J. Simpson case, juror Tracy Hampton went berserk—chewing on a light bulb and biting her arm until it bled.

She was rushed to a hospital, but the day after her release, the pretty twenty-six-year-old flight attendant tried to kill herself by slitting her wrists and had to be hospitalized again.

The story went on to quote ex-juror Katherine Murdock, who was released from the O.J. jury in February, 1995. After describing Tracy as "a sweet, lovely girl, shy and withdrawn . . . (who) stayed alone in her room most of the time," Katherine went on to say: "I don't know what being in jail is like, but being a sequestered juror is really like being a prisoner."

That's Tracy Hampton's story. And it's a lowdown, dirty shame. So if the media wants a story, how about asking why judges and lawyers can trample over our Constitutional rights as Americans when we serve on a jury. Why doesn't the media get upset about American citizens walking into a courthouse to do their jury duty—and suddenly being forced to answer all sorts of questions about their private life? It's illegal, in my opinion. I'm just an average guy who figured The Law would do right by me. When I went through the jury selection process, I just figured it was O.K. for Judge Ito's staff to shove a sixty-one-page questionnaire at me with 294 questions for me to answer. That's right—294 questions! Do they need to pry so deeply into my private life to judge whether or not I'm a fair-minded person who'll do his best to fairly judge a case on the evidence, with the help of eleven other Americans?

Why do I have to reveal potentially embarrassing things about my past, like the so-called "kidnapping" charge that was brought by a jealous girlfriend—and then dropped? What difference does it make that Jeanette Harris had some kind of marital discord back in 1988? Or that one juror went to O.J.'s doctor? Or that another worked for Hertz?

Just try asking O.J. Simpson 294 questions! His lawyers would scream about his right to privacy—and Judge Ito would be listening with a sympathetic ear. You think I'm exaggerating? Well, the whole state of California tried to stop me from writing this book because a politician named Willie Brown concocted a law that says jurors can't get paid for what they write or say. Dove and I went to court and the judge told the state of California that they can't stop me. I have my right of free speech guaranteed under the First Amendment to the Constitution. Yet the state wanted to shut me up. Why? Two people are dead in the O.J. Simpson case. I don't think this book will kill anybody.

And what about O.J. Simpson? Here's a man who's the prime suspect in a brutal murder, yet he was allowed to write a book that protested his innocence right from his jail cell. For profit! And while the People are judging his guilt or innocence!

Jeanette Harris? Here's a woman who went on national TV and made statements that rocked America. She exercised her First Amendment rights and launched a jury probe by Judge Ito that led to the removal of three white deputies—who'll forever be unfairly tarred with the brush of racism. And that led to history's first-known jury revolt. Wow! Are you telling me that's O.K. because she did it for free?

Judge Ito kicked me off the jury. That was embarrassing enough. Then the media got their shot at dragging my name through the mud. In addition to the rumors I've already mentioned, they started whispering that I had impregnated a juror. Try explaining THAT to your wife! Now I think it's my turn. Writing a book is the most complete way to tell the story of the O.J. jury from the inside—and so what if I make a few bucks? Just try doing this sometime. Honesty is painful business, and it'll be the hardest money you've ever earned.

One more point before I climb off my soap box. I've already said that sequestering juries for a long time is a bad idea. Judge Ito tried to make things better, but it was too little, too late. Roger Williams playing piano for a mostly African-American audience? He's a nice man, very talented, and we all appreciated him giving his time. But tinkling out oldies like "Autumn Leaves" wasn't what we needed. That jury would have been a lot happier if we could have relaxed in the hotel bar and had a couple of drinks after a hard day of hanging in the jury room waiting for Darden and Cochran to stop bad-mouthing each other at sidebars.

Here's a warning if you're ever facing jury sequestration: You probably won't be allowed to have so much as one beer no matter how long the trial lasts. That's how we were treated on the O.J. jury—like we were kids who had no rights. If I'd been told during se-

lection process that I couldn't have a pop or
two after work, I'd have quit on the spot. And
remember—we had to beg to get Judge Ito
to allow conjugal visits! What kind of treatment is this? What's the purpose?

There's just one word for it. Bullshit!

Like most average Americans, I didn't
know my rights. I let the court walk all over
me and my right to privacy. And now it's time
for some of these high-priced lawyers, or
judges, or law school professors to come up
with a better way. I don't know if the entire
jury system needs an overhaul. I wasn't
around long enough to form an opinion
about that. But here's what has to happen:
Stop judges and lawyers from trampling on
jurors' rights by asking questions that are nobody's business. A few questions that have to
do with the case itself, fine. Anything else—
hit the road, Jack!

Don't sequester juries. PERIOD! Let
them live at home. People have better judgment than lawyers and judges think. I might
be average, but I'm not stupid. I can live in
my home at night, then attend court in the
morning, and make a fair judgment based on

the evidence. And I'll follow the rules about not discussing the case with family, friends, or neighbors. Sequestering jurors makes them crazy. This case definitely proved that—with sometimes tragic results!

There might be exceptions, such as if you're sitting on a case involving the mob and there's a danger of them coming to your house and offing you. That's when I'll be the first one in favor of court protection. But if you must sequester people, come up with a better way. Don't maker them prisoners if a trial's going to go on forever.

And STOP lawyers from trying to build bias into juries. Using "experts" to fashion a tailor-made jury isn't the American way. I now know that the Sixth Amendment to the Constitution calls for an "impartial jury," not impartial jurors. In the O.J. case, the majority of jurors are African Americans, and that makes people think there will automatically be an acquittal or a hung jury. Well, here's this African American's opinion: Based on the evidence I've heard and seen—particularly the strong blood evidence—I'm leaning toward a verdict of guilty! I'll wait until closing statements, but that's the way I'm leaning. It's how I felt as a juror, and nothing has changed my mind since.

Surprised? So are Chris Darden and Marcia Clark, I'll bet. They had me kicked off the jury because of their "expert" opinion that my Forty-Niners' cap and jacket meant I was hopelessly biased in favor of O.J., no matter what the evidence. I hope O.J. can prove his innocence. But if he's guilty, I'm not going to consider it some kind of defeat for the black race. This case was never about race. Jeanette Harris made the statement on TV that O.J. can't get a fair trial. Not true. Despite the known fact that there are racist cops on the LAPD, O.J. was handled with kid gloves from the start. Legal experts everywhere said that his arrest as prime suspect came at least a couple of days after it should have. And why did he run when offered the chance to turn himself in? O.J.'s getting a fair trial. I was there. I saw it.

And while I'm talking about O.J. getting a fair trial, let me tell you firsthand about the impact of his Dream Team. When you're sitting in that jury box and they're arguing their case right at you . . . Man, what a show! Talk about power and charisma. You don't nod off when Johnnie Cochran, F. Lee Bailey, or Carl Douglas take the floor. It's like something I once heard on a radio interview with famous trial lawyer Gerry Spence—that tall guy who wears buckskin jackets and looks like a cowboy. Once, during a closing argument, Spence walked up to his opponent, a prosecuting attorney, clapped his hands in the guy's face and yelled: "WAKE UP!" That's what it was every time Johnnie and his crew went to work—a wake-up call! My fellow jurors and I would immediately sit up straighter, start paying attention. Believe me—when the Dream Team talked, the O.J. jury listened.

Sure, I've said more than once that the prosecution's powerful evidence impressed me. But the prosecutors themselves? That's another story. Marcia Clark, Christopher Darden, and the rest of the prosecution team had a great case, but they never knew how to present it. They just couldn't keep it sharp and simple. They fumbled and fretted, continually conferring with each other. It was like they were never sure of how to say what they needed to tell us. Sometimes they got it together, but mostly their presentation was truly pathetic; sloppy, badly organized, and rarely eloquent—even though the evidence itself was powerful. And all too often, when the prosecution came up to bat, We the Jury started fidgeting and getting restless.

I heard Christopher Darden say the other day that he'd probably never practice law again once the O.J. trial was over because everything about it was "imperfect." Well, I sure hope he was including himself in that criticism. His remark reflects the cranky, pouting manner he had in court. Darden acted like a big baby, throwing temper tantrums every time he didn't get his way. And his constant battles with Johnnie Cochran were ridiculous. It was pretty obvious that he felt intimidated and outclassed by Johnnie, and wanted to show that he was the better man of the two African-American lawyers in that courtroom. That dirty look he kept aiming at Johnnie was, apparently, his most powerful weapon. But it misfired every time.

Johnnie Cochran? They don't get any

smoother than that—and I know most white people probably assume that black people lean toward him because of race. There may be some truth to that, but I think most African-Americans found F. Lee Bailey to be mighty formidable. And what both lawyers have in common is their ability to give you a story—an interesting narrative—wrapped around their facts. There's a great storytelling tradition in African-American culture, stretching way back to tribal campfires and continuing in this country right through the ordeal of slavery, when black people were forbidden to learn how to read or write. Johnnie and F. Lee have different styles, but they're both great orators. They tell you things in a way that seems to make everything crystal clear. I'm not saying that you necessarily believed every word—but you knew they'd never bore you or confuse you.

Carl Douglas is also a spellbinder. After my dismissal from the jury, I heard one commentator point out that Douglas, during his withering cross-examination of ex-cop Ron Shipp, spoke in the cadences of a black preacher. Amen, brother! You got that right.

Even Robert Shapiro, while not as flamboyant as the others, comes across as very smooth and assured. He makes you feel like there's no sweat, no problem, everything's looking good. The Dream Team cost O.J. millions, but they're worth every penny.

One issue I have not touched on: the Dream Team's police conspiracy theory. Do I believe it? Like most African Americans, I am extremely skeptical of statements and evidence offered by the police. But evidence showed that O.J. got preferential treatment from the LAPD. When Nicole called 911 in 1989, for instance, police found her cowering and badly beaten outside the house and told O.J. to come downtown with them. Instead, O.J. took off in his car. Yet the police took no action. How many black men could have gotten away with ignoring a direct order from street cops? And there's absolutely no doubt O.J. had many white police pals. Don't forget that most of O.J.'s cronies and golfing buddies were middle-aged white men.

Will African Americans vote for O.J.'s innocence even if the evidence proves beyond a shadow of doubt that he's guilty? That's another example of racist thinking. Let me tell you something: I believe jurors can make fair decisions, even if they like or admire a defendant, if the evidence is strong enough. Most people would guess that Jeanette Harris is biased in O.J.'s favor, but I don't know that to be true. I think Jeanette is intelligent enough to make a fair decision based on evidence. I'm leaning toward a guilty verdict, but I could change that opinion in a heartbeat if I see the right evidence. After serving on the O.J. jury—and knowing the players—I guarantee one thing: There's going to be a lively discussion in that jury room. But I'm confident that people with different life backgrounds—and even prejudices—can be basically fair. Lawyers may not believe that there's such a thing as a fair trial by a jury of our peers, but I don't agree. And one reason people have less respect for lawyers than ever these days is because they appear to look down on us, treating us like pawns to be manipulated so that their idea of justice can be served.

Why can't the court call in maybe thirty or forty Americans, make sure they have no direct bias that would influence them in that specific case, then pick twelve jurors and alternates? And if juries must be sequestered, conduct studies to figure out how to make it a reasonably pleasant and dignified experience.

One final word about the history-making jurors' revolt. It made me proud that the majority of the jurors showed up in court wearing black as a protest against three white deputies being removed in the wake of Jeanette Harris's charge of racism. My educated guess is that after I left, poor Tracy Hampton had no one to turn to and—rather than face ostracism—buddied up to Jeanette and the group that kept looking to find fault with the white jurors and deputies: Mr. Johnson, Carl, Fred, and a few others.

After Jeanette's sensational TV interview forced Judge Ito to probe the jury again, I believe that her cronies repeated their claims of white racism—and Tracy's claim of Peeping Toms. The judge overreacted; and as we now know from ousted juror Francine Florio-Bunten, many of the jurors were deeply upset because they'd come to regard these deputies as decent people trying to do a tough job right.

As this final page of my juror "diary" is written, news reports say two more jurors are about to be removed. Let me end, then, with two predictions: Before this history-making trial ends, there will be less than twelve jurors. However, Johnnie Cochran and the prosecution will agree to accept their verdict.

And unless there is an eleventh-hour plea bargain deal made—O.J. Simpson will be convicted of murder.

Prisoner of Justice
by
Pierce O'Donnell

"Nothing worth anything comes without a struggle," a wise teacher once told me. Fighting for what we believe is right—striking a blow for the truth as we see it—is ennobling. And out of the exhilarating collision of fresh thinking and conventional wisdom our souls are purified and social progress is advanced.

No one knows better than Michael Knox and Dove Books what a struggle it has been for this book to be published.

The Private Diary of an O.J. Juror has emerged from a simmering caldron of controversy. After all, it is a book about the most publicized murder prosecution in the annals of American jurisprudence. Orenthal James Simpson—one of America's greatest sports heroes—has been charged with the brutal slayings of his former wife and her friend. Simpson has consistently proclaimed his innocence.

With no witnesses to the crime, the prosecution's case turns on circumstantial evidence. But it is powerful and compelling—Simpson's blood at the murder scene and the victims' blood at his home. In addition, there is evidence of a motive to kill because of a past history of spousal abuse and his all-consuming jealousy, the victims' wounds are consistent with a rage killing, and the defendant had ample opportunity that fateful evening. These are the ingredients of a strong case for the prosecution.

The defense has adopted a "take-no-prisoners" posture. The high-profile defense lawyers challenge virtually every prosecution witness, while arguing that Simpson was framed by racist police officers who planted his blood at the crime scene and the bloody glove at his home. In response to the damning DNA matchups of the blood samples, the defense asserts that inept police criminalists contaminated the blood samples, thereby skewing the positive DNA test results. In other words, the Gang That Couldn't Shoot Straight got its act together long enough to concoct an elaborate conspiracy to pin the murder on a defendant who had many friends in the Los Angeles Police Department.

The pretrial proceedings and the trial have been fraught with sensationalism, scandal, and rumors. Jurors have been dismissed for alleged misconduct, including lying about domestic violence in their backgrounds. The trial lawyers on both sides have been admonished, sanctioned and fined by an alternately indulgent/impatient trial judge. Cameras have invaded the courtroom for gavel-to-gavel television coverage, creating a "media circus." And there is no shortage of "experts" who offer daily commentary—along with a lot of nonsense—about every nuance of the proceedings.

The controversy has been exacerbated by the slow pace of the trial, tedious defense cross-examination, the jurors' work stoppage, reports of personality clashes among jurors, charges that the bailiffs are racists, the dwindling juror pool and the rising risk of a mistrial, unprofessional name-calling by the lawyers, the publication of books by Faye Resnick and Simpson and a book about Kato Kaelin during the trial, and the allegations of police cover-up, racism, and conspiracy. To gain some perspective, it should be remembered that the two dozen surviving Nazi leaders of the Third Reich were prosecuted for countless crimes against humanity at Nuremberg in less time than it will take to prosecute O.J. Simpson.

In the fishbowl of Judge Lance Ito's courtroom, even the slightest glitch or problem is magnified by the instantaneous media reports and the need to fill time during lengthy delays in the taking of testimony. Hyperbole has become commonplace—the defendant has hired the Dream Team for the Trial of the Century. Measured, balanced analysis is in scarce supply.

Nothing comes easy in this case. The simplest act of marking an exhibit or identifying a photograph can be contentious. The prosecution has not presented a crisp case, and the defense delights in the trivialization of the mundane and unsubstantiated charges against the police in the hope of engendering a "reasonable doubt" in at least one juror's mind. Meanwhile, the guilt or innocence of the accused and justice for the victims and their families become more and more secondary as the farce proceeds.

To this spectacle the powers that be in California added yet another bizarre twist. Despite a half-dozen laws that make it a crime to tamper with a jury during a trial, the California legislature passed "the O.J. Law" that prohibits a juror from being paid more than fifty dollars for "any information" about a trial until ninety days after the trial has ended. Read literally, even a juror who has been dismissed and will not deliberate must wait until three months after the trial before he or she can agree to publish a book and accept any advance.

After being sequestered for almost two months, Michael Knox was discharged from the Simpson jury on March 1, 1995. The circumstances of his dismissal were controversial, and he had strong feelings about what he had seen, learned, and experienced from the very first day that he was summoned to the Criminal Courts Building in downtown Los Angeles in the fall of 1994. An ordinary citizen from Long Beach who was a family man and had worked for Federal Express for years, Knox had no literary ambitions. But he did want to tell the public about his six months as a vital participant in the so-called Trial of the Century. Unlike other discharged Simpson jurors, however, Knox was willing to make a substantial time commitment to collaborate on a book. And he understandably wanted to be paid for his efforts.

Dove Books learned of Knox's desire to tell his story. The nation's leading independent audiobook publisher, Dove is also the feisty Los Angeles firm that published Faye Resnick's best-selling account of her friendship with Nicole Brown Simpson and, most recently, released Lyle Menendez's jailhouse taped conversations in a book and companion audio-cassette. Dove wanted to publish Knox's memoirs. Customarily, the parties would sign a publishing contract and the publisher would pay a portion of the advance, the balance to be paid upon completion of the manuscript.

The only problem was that this routine act would be a crime in California under existing law.

Michael Knox's desire to be heard thus unexpectedly thrust him into a battle over freedom of speech, in a battle over the constitutionality of the O.J. Law. In resolving this collision between the constitutional guarantees of free speech and fair trial, the legal system performed at its best. The Founding Fathers created an independent federal judiciary as a check and balance on legislative excesses, particularly those laws that limited our basic civil liberties. They intentionally enshrined the guarantees of free speech and free press in the First Amendment of the Bill of Rights—sending an unambiguous message down through the ages that these precious rights were the foundation stones of American democracy.

―――――――

"The injunction is granted."

With those welcome words from Federal District Court Judge Manuel L. Real on May 29,

1995, Michael Knox and Dove Books cleared the last hurdle to the publication of Knox's book. Technically, the favorable court ruling liberated the book from the stranglehold of California Penal Code Section 116.5, the brand new law criminalizing the publication of any statement "in relation to an action or proceeding" by a former juror in a criminal case until ninety days after the trial was over if the publisher paid more than fifty dollars to the author. Section 116.5 had been hastily enacted last August by the California legislature in a knee-jerk reaction to the media feeding frenzy surrounding *The People v. O.J. Simpson*. Despite warnings from their own staff and the American Civil Liberties Union that the measure abridged free speech rights in violation of the First Amendment to the United States Constitution, the legislators rushed to pass the bill, and Governor Pete Wilson—citing the threat to fair and impartial jury trials—immediately signed it into law.

In late April of this year, Michael Viner, Dove's gutsy president, hired me to advise him about whether he could enter into a contract with, and pay an advance to, Michael Knox. Under Section 116.5, he could not without risking criminal prosecution. However, my team at the Los Angeles Office of Kaye, Scholer, Fierman, Hays & Handler—Clark Kelso, Rex

Reeves, John Shaeffer, and Kym Wulfe—and I immediately concluded that California Penal Code Section 116.5 was unconstitutional. The relevant legal principles were central to freedom of speech in our society.

The First Amendment unequivocally commands that "Congress shall make no law . . . abridging the freedom of speech," and the Supreme Court long ago applied this terse prohibition to the state legislatures. A litany of Supreme Court decisions have ruled that government could not burden speech based on its content. In the free competition of ideas, all voices—no matter how frivolous, offensive, or controversial the message—must be heard. Similarly, government cannot draw a distinction between speakers or writers who are being paid as opposed to those who speak or write for free. In other words, "free speech" does not mean that it must be uncompensated to be accorded First Amendment protection. And any delay imposed on the exercise of free speech rights, no matter how slight, is suspect.

While we believed that the law was unenforceable, we had to devise a strategy that both gave Knox and Dove some comfort that they would not be spending Christmas in prison and cleared the way for publication in the next six weeks. Put another way, merely because we felt that the law was unconstitutional did not mean that we could win at all, much less that we could have the law invalidated fast enough for Dove to publish the book, given the limited window of time that Dove saw for an ex–O.J. juror book. In addition, a case that dragged on for months—or years as I have learned the hard way—would be too expensive for the client. Justice delayed is not only justice denied—it's unaffordable.

Kaye, Scholer's assignment therefore was to get a successful result in a few weeks and at a cost that did not eat up all the profits from Knox's book.

One option was to go ahead, sign the contract, and announce that we planned to publish the book and wait for the Los Angeles County district attorney, Gil Garcetti, to prosecute. The three disadvantages with this wait-and-see approach were that we would be on the defensive, a state court is not always the most hospitable forum for federal constitutional arguments, and we needed a quick resolution. In addition, Knox and his savvy attorney, Arthur Barens, were understandably reluctant to defy the law.

Another alternative was to try to persuade Garcetti, a bright, thoughtful prosecutor, that the statute was unconstitutional and that he should not prosecute. I called him and made my pitch. Politely but emphatically, he told me that his office had supported the legislation and that he would "aggressively" prosecute Dove and Knox if they went ahead with the book. I believed him.

The only other option—filing a lawsuit in federal court seeking a preliminary injunction—had its own disadvantages. There was no guarantee that we could get an expedited hearing, and the government might successfully get our case bounced to state court, citing Supreme Court precedent cautioning restraint when federal courts are asked to enjoin a threatened state prosecution. While we could argue that federal courts are not supposed to abstain nor defer to state judges when First Amendment liberties are at stake, I could not assure Dove that we would get a speedy trial.

We had another problem.

While judges are supposed to decide cases on their own merits, they are human beings who read newspapers and watch the evening television news. Like everyone else, judges are "O.J. junkies." Any federal judge assigned our case would be intimately familiar with the case and all the attendant controversy about the trial, particularly about the behavior of jurors, the public statements of dismissed jurors (especially Jeanette Harris), the intrusive effect of cameras in the courtroom, and the growing public disenchantment with the length of the trial, the sensationalism, and the behavior of the lawyers and Judge Lance Ito. Against this backdrop, the state's anticipated arguments— that the new criminal law was necessary to avoid the appearance of impropriety and to deter jurors from trying to make a quick buck by being dismissed—might strike a responsive chord with a federal judge.

On our advice, Dove decided to take the initiative. Knox agreed to be a co-plaintiff, and we filed suit on April 12, 1995, naming as primary defendants California Attorney General Daniel Lungren, the state's chief law enforcement officer, and District Attorney Gil Garcetti. The case was assigned to Judge Richard Gadbois, a former state court trial judge who had been appointed to the federal bench by President Ronald Reagan in 1982. A hearing was set for May 15, 1995.

The Attorney General, joined by Garcetti, filed a vigorous opposition to our attack on the statute. The very integrity of the jury process and the defendant's right to a fair and impartial trial were at stake, the defendants argued. The suspension of Knox's free speech rights—until ninety days after the trial ended—was necessary to serve these compelling state interests. Otherwise, they contended, jurors would be tempted by distractions like lucrative book and TV interview deals. This "juror journalism" could be stopped only if we eliminated the temptation and had a "cooling off" period after the trial.

These were weighty arguments advanced with the utmost sincerity. There was a surface attraction to the state's contention that the exercise of free speech was not being suppressed, but only delayed, and that the temporary suspension of one man's freedom was a small price to pay for the greater good of protecting the constitutional rights of O.J. Simpson and all criminal defendants. Nonlawyers whom I polled felt strongly that there was something unseemly about jurors writing books at all, much less former jurors cashing in on their jury service while the trial was still proceeding. We would ignore the visceral appeal of this argument at our peril.

In our rebuttal brief, we pointed out that the state had failed to show that the means chosen to accomplish these concededly important interests was as unintrusive of First Amendment rights as possible. Put another way, the defendants, we asserted, had not overcome our argument that this law was legislative overkill and was not narrowly tailored to avoid unnecessary abridgement of free speech. For example, while we readily agreed that the statute could prohibit sitting jurors from entering into book deals while the trial was in progress, we questioned how it advanced the goal of a fair and impartial jury to silence a former juror who would not deliberate—especially where the jury was sequestered. We also noted that the legislature had failed to outlaw other vital participants from writing a book during the trial. Indeed, as the trial was getting underway, Simpson had published a best-selling and highly lucrative book protesting his innocence.

We had another line of attack: The court should not blithely assume, as the state alleged, that there was in fact a problem with jurors being distracted from their duties by the lure of capitalizing on their jury service. The state had offered only speculation or anecdotes, and the only comprehensive study of the issue had concluded that there was no empirical evidence of a problem.

The stage was set for a constitutional showdown on May 15. Unfortunately, when we arrived at the courtroom, we learned that Judge Gadbois was ill and that the hearing would be postponed. This was not only a letdown for the lawyers who had prepared to argue, but it meant more delay for Dove. The book was scheduled to go to the printer within a matter of weeks, but no contract had been signed.

The motion for preliminary injunction was reassigned to Judge Manuel Real, the former chief judge for the Central District of California, and the hearing was set for May 22. Our computer-assisted legal research did not turn up any significant reported First Amendment decisions by Judge Real. As we went to court that morning, I had no inkling of where he might be leaning.

I quickly learned.

Only a few minutes into my opening argument, Judge Real observed, "Mr. O'Donnell, the integrity of the jury system is a compelling state interest."

I had my work cut out for me, it seemed.

Agreeing with the veteran jurist, I pointed out that California had plenty of statutes that punished jury tampering, adding, "But Michael Knox no longer sits. He served as a citizen, as an officer of the court, if you will, fifty days and then was discharged."

"But he was a sitting juror?" Judge Real asked.

"No question he sat on that case," I answered. "He no longer sits. He has no ability whatsoever legally to influence the thinking of his former colleagues or their deliberations. . . . This jury, as you know, . . . is sequestered. So the book that Michael Knox wants to write and the book that my client wants to publish will never be read by those jurors until their service is over."

Judge Real was not persuaded.

"The integrity of the jury system goes beyond that, doesn't it, Mr. O'Donnell, goes beyond the fact of, quote, influencing the jury?"

The judge was concerned about the appearance of impropriety of former jurors writing books while the case on which they served was still pending. I turned to our argument that mere "undifferentiated or generalized speculation of harm" will not justify the denial of free speech. I also noted that two states, New York and New Jersey, had legislated in this area, but they regulated only sitting jurors and imposed no waiting period after the trial ends.

I cited the Supreme Court's unanimous decision in 1991 invalidating New York's "Son of Sam" law that required criminals to forfeit proceeds from books they wrote about their crimes and pay the money to a fund for their victims. But Judge Real noted that the Simon & Schuster case was readily distinguishable from a ninety-day limitation because New York's law imposed a five-year limitation on a publication which was "for all intents and purposes" a total ban.

I could tell that I was not persuading the only person who counted. So I shifted gears. Over the weekend, I had just read the first third of Knox's manuscript, and I was impressed with his candor and observations about jury selection, sequestration, racism, and the impact of the trial on him and others. I wanted to persuade Judge Real that Michael Knox had not only a right to be heard, but that we had a need to hear what he had to say.

> I want to talk about something else. There is a competing First Amendment value here. . . . Judge [Shirley] Hufstedler, for whom I clerked many years ago in this courthouse and whom this court knows well, once said that, when government trenches upon First Amendment values, it must use a scalpel, and not an ax. . . . The legislature . . . engaged in legislating with an ax here, and their staff told them that.

> This is an unusual, extraordinary trial. Some say it's the Trial of the Century. But it is a criminal trial, and Michael Knox has things to say about his jury service. . . .

> As an African-American male, your Honor, he has things to say that are important. He has things to say about pretrial publicity, about jury sequestration. He has things to say about the efficacy of the criminal justice system, how jurors are treated. . . . He has a right under the First Amendment . . . to write that, and Dove has a right to publish it.

"Those are all things that he can do later," Judge Real interjected. "Same thing with the same effect."

I argued that the Supreme Court had consistently ruled that any delay in the exercise of free speech was presumed to be unconstitutional. When Arthur Barens got up to argue, Judge Real pressed the point: "It's not a loss [of free speech and free press], it's a postponement. . . . It is not a violation of the right."

Barens cited the Simon & Schuster case, but Judge Real felt that the case had to be understood in light of a five-year restriction, and not a brief postponement until a trial is finished. When Barens argued that the Simpson jury was sequestered and out of harm's way, Judge Real gave a hint of what he thought of the proceedings a few blocks from his courthouse: "The integrity of the sitting jury goes beyond the Simpson case. It may die with the Simpson case, but it goes beyond."

Judge Real wondered aloud whether the fact that Knox was being paid—as opposed to "doing it altruistically to change the system"— was a relevant consideration. But the issue that captured his imagination more than anything else was timing.

"Putting aside the First Amendment, tell

me why it has to be published now. What is it
about 'now' that it must be published?"

Barens told the court that "the interest is
at its peak now. . . ." It was a good answer, but
Judge Real did not seem persuaded.

I rose to take a stab at answering his jugu-
lar question:

> I guess the most fundamental tenet of the
> First Amendment that we learned in law
> school, which [Justice Oliver Wendell]
> Holmes talked about, is the free competi-
> tion of ideas in a public forum. We've got
> a former juror . . . named Jeanette Harris,
> an African-American female.

> She left the jury; she was discharged.
> Went on a press, media interview tour.
> She made very serious allegations about
> the sheriffs, about racism and other
> things. Michael Knox wants to write now,
> while it is timely, to enter that forum and
> to answer her, and he will if his book is
> published. That is the best answer to why
> now. Months from now, when this trial
> hopefully ends some day, there won't be
> as much interest in that. Public interest—

"He can go out and talk," the judge interjected. "There's nobody stopping him from
talking."

"Yes, but the First Amendment jurisprudence is as clear as my nose is Irish," I interjected with a smile, "that you can't punish speech merely because it's compensated." Grinning from my attempt at self-deprecating humor, Judge Real nodded almost imperceptibly. I tried to drive the point home.

> Let Michael Knox, for his nonaltruistic reasons perhaps . . . enter the forum. He's writing the book. It's not like he's doing nothing. He's working for it [his money]. He has important things to say. The Attorney General can't be the censor. The legislature can't be. Don't let the state make you the censor of whether Michael Knox can get those views out there. I've read a portion of the manuscript. Let Michael Knox speak!

The argument continued for almost another hour. The Attorney General's counsel, Paul Dobson, repeated all of the arguments in his opposing brief. Judge Real was particularly concerned about the ninety-day waiting period. When Dobson suggested that this was a necessary "cooling off period," the judge wanted to know "cooling off from what?" Dobson suggested that it reduced the temptation to sell the story. When the trial court pressed harder, the state's argument seemed to reduce to the proposition that the value of the story diminished with time—the very point that Barens and I had tried to make.

Judge Real also took aim at the absence of any studies supporting the need for a 90-day cooling off period and the arbitrariness of selecting 90 as opposed to 30 or 120 days. When Dobson picked up on my imagery of the scalpel and ax, Judge Real could not resist.

"Who was wielding the scalpel to say ninety days was enough to cut it out?"

When Dobson argued that ninety days was "the margin that just cut around" the problem, the judge skewered him.

"If the doctor is going to use a scalpel on me, I hope that he has an X-ray to find out where it's going to be."

The judge was making our argument that remedial legislation aimed at preventing jury tampering in the form of jurors signing book contracts had to pinpoint the problem and draw a close connection between the cure and the problem. If the concern was financial temptation of sitting jurors, the law should reach only them and not draw within its dragnet discharged jurors and not extend the suspension of free speech one minute longer than necessary.

Counsel for District Attorney Garcetti,

Richard Townsend, argued passionately that he knew that there was "a very severe problem that threatens the very core of the jury system in this county" because of jurors wanting to make money off of their jury service. This revelation was not based on any empirical studies, but rather on Townsend's recent personal experience as a criminal juror and talking to lots of non–O.J. jurors in the jury assembly room on the same ninth floor of the Criminal Courts Building where the Simpson case is being tried. "The jurors talked of nothing else other than making money," he assured us.

After my objection that counsel was improperly testifying, Judge Real took over again. He doubted that there was any way for prospective jurors to manipulate the system so that they could be assigned to courtrooms with high-profile (and potentially lucrative) cases. When Townsend argued that it was a matter of common sense knowledge, the judge insisted on concrete evidence that this was in fact happening. The county's counsel had none.

Following brief rebuttal arguments, the judge unfolded his decision. He was not persuaded that Section 116.5 was unconstitutional on its face. In other words, under some circumstances, the law might be validly applied—for example, as we conceded, to a sitting juror during the trial. The ninety-day waiting period troubled him, but he did not have to decide that issue today.

The judge was convinced, however, that the statute was unconstitutional as applied to Michael Knox who was no longer a juror and could not affect the jury's deliberations. Judge Real would enter an injunction against enforcement of the law against Knox and Dove. We had won.

The state did not ask the judge to stay his decision so that it could take an immediate appeal. The injunction was therefore effective from the moment it was announced by the court. Within hours of our victory, Knox signed his publishing contract with Dove and received his advance. The next day, the state told us that it might take an emergency appeal to reverse the injunction. As this book goes to press a week after the ruling, Judge Real's injunction is still in place.

Whether the struggle to publish this book was worth the effort remains for the reader to determine. I must confess that I thoroughly enjoyed *The Private Diary of an O.J. Juror*. If for no other reason, I learned how an intelligent layperson reacts to America's criminal justice system. For that reason alone, I believe that Michael Knox's book has something terribly important to say about what is good and what needs changing in the process by which we adjudicate criminal cases.

A personal memoir of an ordinary citizen summoned to serve on the jury of *The People v. O.J. Simpson*, this book is a frank account of Knox's background, his troubled youth and brushes with the law when he lived in San Diego, his new life as a family man in Long Beach, his personal experiences with racism at Federal Express where he worked for years, his impressions of what might become the Mistrial of the Century, the tensions—racial and otherwise—among jurors, and the vicissitudes of sequestration. More than anything else, what distinguishes this book is Michael Knox's distinctive voice—he comes across as an honest, vulnerable man who took his juror duties seriously, but who got dismissed for failing to give a complete account in his juror questionnaire about his arrest record.

Knox's most redeeming quality as an author is that he's unpretentious: "Telling my story is the scariest thing that I've ever done. . . . I'm just an average guy, working two jobs, trying to feed my family and have a decent life."

At one point as the trial is getting underway, Knox reflects on his awesome responsibility as a juror:

> Here's a man on trial for a horrible crime and I've been chosen to sit in judgment of him. This isn't play-acting. It's as serious as life gets. I just hope I can do a good job. God, don't let me make any mistakes.

The value of Knox's story is not diminished by his abbreviated stay on the jury. Nearly two months of hearing opening statements and testimony and sequestration, preceded by several months of *voir dire* and waiting for the trial to commence, give him more than sufficient experiences to express his opinions. Indeed, when I finished the book, I wished that Knox was still a juror so that we could get his take on the rest of the trial and the jury's deliberations. More important, I felt that the prosecution and defense were shortchanged by Knox's dismissal because he comes across as a conscientious juror who would have emerged as a leader in the jury room.

Knox pulls no punches in his critique of the callous treatment of jurors in high-profile cases. He rails against the "illegal" sixty-one-page juror questionnaire with 294 questions about some of the most private facts about his life—"stuff that has nothing to do with whether or not I'm a fair-minded person who'll do his best to listen and make a judgment along with eleven other Americans." In Knox's view, "Now it's time for some of these high-priced lawyers, or judges, or law school professors to come up with a better way."

Knox saves his harshest denunciation for sequestration. It is difficult for anyone who has not served for months on a sequestered jury to understand the isolation and hardships, and in the Simpson case, they were compounded. Like the lawyers, judge, and witnesses, the jurors have become celebrities, subject to invasive media coverage, unfounded rumors, and outright defamation. Unlike all the other players, however, the jurors are sequestered and far less able to protect themselves. Indeed, a comparison of the restrictions on the jurors living in a first-class Los Angeles hotel and O.J. Simpson residing in the Los Angeles County jail shows that, while the accommodations are different, the defendant actually enjoys more freedom than his peers sitting in judgment of him.

Michael Knox starts off with much enthusiasm about his mission, describing the twenty-four strangers who were jurors and alternates as "a team for justice." But the harsh effects of sequestration quickly take their toll. The posh hotel surroundings could not overcome the feeling of "a military boot camp"—early wake-up, hurry-up-and-wait, marching in single file everywhere, no privacy, room searches, boring routine, and isolation from the rest of the world. These private citizens were literally drafted out of their normal lives—legally kidnapped from family, friends, and work. It is hardly surprising that they became stir crazy and, in one case, even suicidal.

"Now I know what O.J. must feel like," Knox writes on only the second day of sequestration.

Knox and his fellow jurors became prisoners of justice. He complains:

> No one in the court system had leveled with us. It's not that they were trying to hide the truth. After all, we knew that we'd be locked away in a hotel, isolated from family and friends, possibly without conjugal visits. But nobody emphasized that we'd actually be worse off than prison inmates, with deputies monitoring not just our activities, but our conversations. . . . Big Brother . . . eavesdropping on every word you utter. It was devastating. . . . Paranoia was everywhere.

After two weeks, Judge Ito granted the jury's request for conjugal visits—five hours on Saturday evening—and Family Day on Sunday.

This mitigated but hardly eliminated the jurors' feelings of isolation and confinement. Nothing else changed; they remained imprisoned in their jury box and hotel rooms.

In the vast majority of criminal cases, juries are not sequestered. It is only the exceptional—and high-profile—prosecutions that warrant this drastic action. (For example, the jury in the Charles Manson case was sequestered for eight and one-half months.) Yet these are the cases most likely to attract massive media attention and shape the public's perception about the effectiveness of the criminal justice system. If a case like *People v. O.J. Simpson* garners negative press about the conduct of the jurors and their lack of candor in their questionnaire responses, many people will believe that this is normal behavior by all jurors—an absolutely erroneous conclusion based on the experience of many of my fellow trial lawyers and myself.

Michael Knox's extremely negative reaction to sequestration is hardly unique. Common sense tells us that it is a sadistic form of cruel and unusual punishment for men and women who are rendering a vital public service for only five dollars per day. In *The Trial of Dr. Spock*, Jessica Mitford describes as "an unrelieved nightmare" one juror's revulsion over only one month of sequestration in the 1968

federal prosecution of the famous pediatrician/
author and four others for conspiracy to counsel, aid, and abet violations of the Selective Service Act. The juror's description of his life in
sequestration mirrors Michael Knox's observations:

'We were permitted to call home once a
day. The calls were monitored—a marshal
was listening in taking notes. Our letters
were censored. . . . All telephones, radios,
and television sets in the bedrooms were
disconnected'. . . . [The juror] hated
being separated from his family, he
missed them terribly. Worst of all was the
regimentation, the lack of activity, constantly waiting around. 'It was atro-
cious. . . . I would kill myself if I ever
ended up in jail in these conditions.'

Michael Knox offers a solution.

Don't sequester juries—PERIOD! Let
them live at home. People have better
judgment than lawyers and judges think.
I might be average, but I'm not stupid. I
can live in my home at night, then go attend court in the morning and make a fair
judgment based on the evidence. And I'll
follow the rules about not discussing the

case with family, friends, or neighbors. Sequestering jurors makes them crazy.

Those who care about the survival of the five-hundred-year-old institution of trial by jury should heed Michael Knox's warning. After the Simpson case, it will be even more difficult to find people who are willing to sacrifice months of their lives for a process that pays them little money and even less respect. We need to pause and reflect on how things have gotten so out of control.

A criminal defendant is constitutionally entitled to a fair and impartial jury. In cases like the Simpson trial, the Oklahoma City federal building bombing, and others involving notorious crimes, it is impossible to find prospective jurors who have not heard about the events at issue. Yet we routinely impanel them, accepting their promise that they will render their verdict solely on the evidence presented in the courtroom and not what they heard or read before the trial.

Sequestration is the most radical measure devised to prevent contamination of the jury during trial from media coverage of the trial. Is it too high a price to pay? Is Michael Knox right when he tells us that we should trust jurors to honor their oath and not be influenced by the press or family and friends? These are questions that not only lawyers and judges but the public at large will ignore at their peril. Michael Knox has rendered an important public service in writing this thought-provoking book.

Let the public debate on reform begin.

Michael Knox is currently living in Southern California with his wife Beverly and their children. He works for Federal Express. He's an avid musician, whose love for life and music keeps the youthful spark in his eyes. He loves to work on cars. His best Saturdays are spent in junk yards looking for priceless 1950s auto parts.

Mike Walker's weekly column in the *National Enquirer* is read by millions. His national radio talk show is syndicated by Westwood One Entertainment. He is the author of the #1 *New York Times* best-seller *Nicole Brown Simpson: The Private Diary of a Life Interrupted* and *The Private Diary of Lyle Menendez*. He currently resides in Palm Beach, Florida.

Roy Innis has been the National Chairman of the Congress of Racial Equality (CORE) for over a quarter of a century. He was the first Ford Foundation fellow at the Metropolitan Applied Research Center, after leaving a career in pharmaceutical and medical research. True to his principles of truth, logic, and courage, he abhors racism of any kind by anyone—regardless of color. His involvement in human rights, victims' rights, education and welfare reform issues span his entire career. In 1993 he ran a strong campaign in a bid to become New York City's second black mayor.

———

Pierce O'Donnell clerked for Supreme Court Justice Byron R. White and spent three years working with legendary trial lawyer Edward Bennett Williams. One of the nation's leading trial lawyers, O'Donnell is a senior partner at Kaye, Scholer, Fierman, Hays & Handler in Los Angeles. He is the co-author of the best-seller *Fatal Subtraction*, and he was a contributor to *The Private Diary of Lyle Menendez*.

———

Bill Robles has been an award-winning freelance courtroom illustrator since 1969 when he covered the Charles Manson trial. Since then he has covered many trials including those of Patricia Hearst, Roman Polansky, and Carol Burnett. He is currently covering the Trial of the Century.